PRAISE FOR WH

M000082055

Charlotte Smith was a tremendous basketball player and now she is one of the bright young coaches in our game. When you read her devotionals, you will understand the passion that drives her purpose. She has a unique way of blending the truth of Scripture and the wisdom they offer to all coaches, whether basketball, soccer or any sport. Refreshing. Challenging. Passionate with purpose. Full of wisdom for all coaches. I will be enjoying this devotional for a long time and giving it to many of my coaching friends.

JANE ALBRIGHT, Head Women's Basketball Coach, University of Nevada, Reno

When choosing sides in a pickup basketball game, you can easily pick the players who are surprised when they make a shot. I want the ones who are surprised when they miss a shot. That's why I choose to recommend Charlotte Smith's new devotional *When Coaches Pray*. She is surprised when God doesn't answer her prayers, not when He does. You can learn from this woman. You want her on your team.

JAY CARTY, Former Los Angeles Lakers Player and Coauthor with John Wooden of *Coach Wooden's Pyramid of Success*

I have known Charlotte Smith for more than 20 years, and am honored to call her a friend. When she played for me at the University of North Carolina, she was a leader on and off the court. She led Bible studies and encouraged everyone to reach for excellence during her days as an assistant at UNC. I have been blessed to watch her grow professionally and spiritually. Her faith is real and so are the devotional readings in this book. *When Coaches Pray* will inspire coaches and leaders everywhere.

SYLVIA HATCHELL, Head Women's Basketball Coach, University of North Carolina

Playing sports all of my life, I have found that the coach is the key to success. Reaching the Super Bowl was a great accomplishment for me and my team. I have a desire to be a coach one day. *When Coaches Pray* will be in my library as I lead young men.

DANIEL KILGORE, NFL Player, San Francisco 49ers

Charlotte was my coach at UNC. Not only was she a great coach, but she was also a great leader, an inspiration and most importantly, a Godly example for us to follow. As a professional basketball player, the need to stay focused and grounded is so vital to continued success. *When Coaches Pray* will help anyone wanting to gain an edge.

LEAH METCALF, Women's Professional Basketball Player, Energy Ivanovo, Russia

Charlotte Smith has had tremendous success as a player, assistant coach and now as a head coach. Her knowledge will now be available for many to read in her book *When Coaches Pray*.

MIKE METCALF, #15 Pit Crew Team, Michael Waltrip Racing

I was Charlotte's host when she came to visit the University of North Carolina as a recruit. Within 30 minutes of our first encounter, I learned that she was musically inclined, hilariously funny, creatively gifted, incredibly witty and a pastor's daughter. Since that time we have been collegiate and professional teammates, roommates, head coaches, seminary graduates and kindred sisters. Over the years, I have witnessed first-hand God's love, grace and mercy flow through her. She has always loved reading the Bible, and has inherited from her father, the late Ulysses Smith, a special gift to rightly divide the Word of God. *When Coaches Pray* is invaluable to coaches who have so much on their plate yet yearn to keep God at the forefront of their lives. This affirming message of hope, faith and healing is a must read for coaches as well as any leader. A gem to be treasured.

SYLVIA CRAWLEY MILBRY, Former WNBA Player, Former Head Coach and Coaching Consultant

We are all coaches, whether it be in our households, businesses or communities. Coaching is all about being good stewards of those whom we lead. Since everyone is a coach at some level, everyone will enjoy and benefit from *When Coaches Pray*.

ROBERT WALKER, Publisher, *Sports Spectrum* Magazine

Charlotte Smith makes a difference in the lives of everyone she touches. As a WNBA player, she was a catalyst that sparked her teammates to excel. As a college coach, she is a servant leader who helps her players to grow. Now with this book she shows what a difference prayer makes in the lives of coaches who want to make a difference in the lives of others—coaches like you.

PAT WILLIAMS, Vice President, Orlando Magic and Author, *The Difference You Can Make*

FOREWORD BY **DAVID THOMPSON**

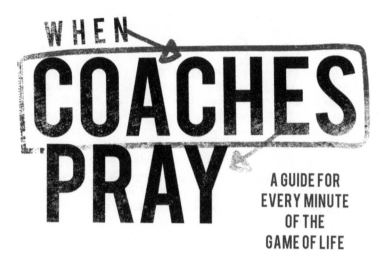

WHEN COACHES PRAY

A GUIDE FOR
EVERY MINUTE
OF THE
GAME OF LIFE

CHARLOTTE D. SMITH

THE
CORE MEDIA
GROUP
™

For more information, email us at
WHENCOACHESPRAY@GMAIL.COM

Published by The Core Media Group
Indian Trail, North Carolina, U.S.A.
publisher@thecoremediagroup.com
www.thecoremediagroup.com
Printed in the U.S.A.

Cover and Interior Design by Rob Williams
rob.insideoutdesign@cox.net

Library of Congress Cataloging-in-Publication Data
(Applied for)

CONTENTS

Foreword by David Thompson...7

Introduction: Hungry to Touch God..9

A Conversation with Charlotte Smith.......................................11

First Half

20:00 Are You Sent? 15

19:00 Overcoming the Fear Factor 17

18:00 Why Coach?...19

17:00 At Your Service...21

16:00 What Is in a Name? 23

15:00 What Are You Saying? 25

14:00 What Are You Hearing?.. 27

13:00 The Cost of Making an Assumption 29

12:00 Back in Bounds...31

11:00 A Triple Threat 33

10:00 Are You Prepared?...35

09:00 Ready to Assist 37

08:00 You Cannot Do It Alone 39

07:00 Insults and Blessings..41

06:00 God Is with You..43

05:00 Light, Camera, Action 45

04:00 Follow Through on Your Promises 47

03:00 Be Christlike..49

02:00 You Are Capable...52

01:00 A Season of Refreshing...55

Halftime

Questions to Ponder 57

Second Half

20:00   A Fresh Start..61

19:00   Where Are You? 63

18:00   Spiritual Fitness 65

17:00   It Is Written 67

16:00   Eyes on the Target 69

15:00   Remain Unshakable 71

14:00   Riding Through the Storm.. 73

13:00   Rebounding.. 75

12:00   Hidden Potential 78

11:00   Stretch, Not Stress 80

10:00   Look Out Below 82

09:00   Good and Teach 84

08:00   Mighty in Battle... 87

07:00   A Heart Transplant.. 90

06:00   The Cost of Loyalty 92

05:00   Mustard Seed Faith 94

04:00   A Reflection of You 96

03:00   A Cover-Up 98

02:00   Not a Substitute 100

01:00   Becoming a Real Champion... 103

00:00   How Will You Be Remembered? 105

Angels Along the Way 107

About the Author.. 110

FOREWORD

BY DAVID THOMPSON

For as long as I can remember, Charlotte Smith has been special. Not just because she grew up in a house with all boys, but also in the way she carried herself from a young age. She was always very smart, had a great sense of humor, and was quite competitive. I know, because as her uncle, I watched her grow up to become the wonderful woman she is today.

I remember the times I came back to Shelby, North Carolina, during my days of playing in the NBA. I would have various competitions with my nieces and nephews. Sometimes we would see who could hold their breath the longest. Other times it was to see who could sit up against the wall the longest. No matter the contest, Charlotte would always win.

I remember when Charlotte won the state championship in the mile wearing a pair of Keds™—and she was only a freshman in high school. As a sophomore she could dunk a basketball, which is totally amazing even to me—and I was known as "the Skywalker."

My only regret is that Charlotte went to play basketball for the North Carolina Tar Heels instead of the North Carolina State Wolfpack (my alma mater). But it is amazing how our careers were so similar. We both had one dunk in a college game. Her dunk was legal, and mine was not (due to the no-dunking rule that existed back then).

Since I attended North Carolina State, the only time I ever rooted for the Tar Heels to win was when Charlotte played there. One of the most exciting moments for me in basketball was when she hit a three-pointer at the buzzer to win the only women's national championship in North Carolina history. Our teams both won a national championship, mine in 1974 and Charlotte's in 1994. We both were All-Americans, Player of the Year, and have had our jersey numbers retired.

In another curious coincidence, we both started our professional careers in Denver. I played for the Nuggets and she played for the Colorado Xplosion. The hand of God had to be in there somewhere.

Charlotte has always been very serious about God. I recall one time when she was required to recite Bible verses. Wanting to be the first to have one memorized, in typical Charlotte fashion, she picked the shortest passage: "Jesus wept" (John 11:35). Jesus probably smiled.

As Charlotte has grown both spiritually and professionally, her faith is very evident in her everyday walk. Her works reflect her faith as she is a faithful servant, and everyone she touches is better for it.

It would be an honor to play for a coach with the knowledge, experience, faith and integrity of Charlotte Smith. May God continue to bless her as she has an increasing impact on many lives for Christ with her book.

We all love Charlotte very much!

CHARLOTTE D. SMITH

Introduction

HUNGRY TO TOUCH GOD

This book is written to coaches and aspiring coaches everywhere. My game is basketball, but yours may be softball, football, soccer, tennis, lacrosse or something else. No matter your sport, as a coach, you have a platform. This means that you have great influence in the lives of both players and fans.

As a Christian, your impact takes on an importance beyond X's and O's. When you honor God and display the character traits of Christ, you draw others into His kingdom. You will in a small way sway people you don't know—perhaps some whom you will see in the stands at games—and you will also inspire complete strangers. But your greatest influence will be in the lives of the players you coach. As you develop relationships with them, you can help build them not only as athletes but also as disciples (I will explain this as I go along).

To positively affect others with any degree of success, you must first choose how you will live your own life. You must be grounded in the Word of God, but each day you also need to nurture and grow your faith. Start by asking yourself some pertinent questions: Do you desire to touch God? Do you seek to establish and maintain a vibrant relationship with Him? Do you pursue His glory above everything else?

With busy schedules—especially during the season—it can be difficult to find personal one-on-one time with God. If you are like me, sometimes it seems that the more I need to hear from Him, the less time I have to be in His Word, in prayer and in worship.

I have written this book to help.

A devotional doesn't replace Bible reading, listening to God's voice or fellowship, but it can encourage you to press forward in your faith. It can help stabilize and grow your relationship with God so that you can always be a positive influence on others. And it can help maintain a little spiritual sanity in the midst of a hectic season!

I have written 41 short, biblically-based readings especially for coaches who follow Jesus, like you and me. You will be inspired to live with great passion and to serve others as you lead them.

Since I am a basketball coach, I have arranged the readings following the 40 minutes of a basketball game: one reading for each minute and one for after the game. Each reading opens with a Scripture and a short *Warm-Up* thought, which is a maxim or truth that will help you gain focus. The *Game Time* and *Timeout* sections that follow expand upon a primary point, direct you to helpful Bible verses, and nudge you to dig a little deeper. The closing *Prayer Time* will help you take the message to heart. Finally, I have included *Clipboard Notes* at the end of each reading. This is space where you can jot down your own thoughts, as God speaks to you. No matter your sport, you can easily follow this simple format, and you will find the messages applicable to your life as a coach. After all, God's Word is for everyone.

I urge you to join me on this journey and to commit 41 days to becoming the coach that God has called you to be. I hope you enjoy the readings, and I pray that you will be challenged to live each day in a way that is pleasing to Christ.

WHEN COACHES PRAY

Q: *When you were growing up, did your family attend church?*

CS: Yes, my father was a pastor and my mother was a missionary. They were both very active in the church. I have a lineage of ministers and pastors on my dad's side of the family. His mother was a minister and his father was a deacon in the church.

Q: *What was your childhood impression of God? Did you see Him as a father figure? Were you afraid of Him?*

CS: As a child, I knew that I needed to be saved or I would spend eternity in hell. Knowing God was more about avoiding hell than building an intimate relationship with a loving Father. I was never afraid of God, but I surely was afraid of going to hell. But as I came to know the heart of my heavenly Father, I came to realize that He wants us to have a relationship based on love and not on fear.

Q: *When was the first time you prayed to God?*

CS: A lot of my early prayers were need-based prayers. I was always asking Him to give me something. As I got to know Him better and experienced more of His love, I started praying with a heart of gratitude, always giving thanks.

Q: *When did you receive Christ as Lord and Savior? How did this change and later affect your life?*

CS: I received Christ as a teenager. There was no instant perfection, but my relationship with Him has steadily grown over the years. It took many disappointments, bumps and bruises for me to fully surrender my will and desires to Him.

Q: *As an athlete, did you pray for your training? Winning? Teammates? Opponents?*

CS: I did pray for training, my health and my teammates. I was surely praying during the National Championship game. I was actually out on the floor during the game throwing my hands up to heaven in praise! When I made a three-point play, I would lift my hands up right there on the court and say, "Thank You, Lord."

I remember chapel in the WNBA. Chapel was important to a lot of players and for whatever reason chapel was discontinued in New York. So I decided when we got there that we would have chapel on the court since we no longer had a room nor a chaplain. We gathered on the court and prayed. When I became a free agent, New York was interested in signing me. I remember talking with the general manager about the possibility, but I said there was one problem. I told her that I could not come to New York because the team didn't have chapel. It was in my search for a new team in the WNBA that God was able to use me for His glory and restore chapel services to the New York Liberty.

Q: *When did you come to realize the importance of prayer?*

CS: I have always known the importance of prayer because I grew up seeing the results of prayer in my home. My parents were praying people. Over the years, as my prayer life has evolved, I now understand more because of the intimacy that I have with God through prayer. At my home church, Life International, in Durham, North Carolina, we have all-night prayer services on Friday nights. They run from 11:30 P.M. to 6:00 A.M. Prayer is important.

Q: *How has God answered your prayers as a player and as a coach?*

CS: I remember one time when I was playing basketball for USA Basketball. I tore my hamstring completely the night before the championship game horse-playing in the hallway of the hotel. I heard it pop; it sounded like a firecracker. I could not even walk back to my room. My teammates had to assist me. Right before the game the next day I was walking around in a circle praying out to God from the depths of my heart. And with each lap in my prayer circle I could feel myself moving towards victory! I played that game and received MVP of the tournament! God is faithful even when we almost blow it!

God answered my prayers because as a child I wanted to play basketball. He blessed me with the talent, skills and ability to do so. As a coach, He has given me the opportunity to touch the lives of so many people. This was my prayer, to be able to impact lives for His glory.

20:00
19:00
18:00
17:00
16:00
15:00
14:00
13:00

FIRST HALF

12:00
11:00
10:00
09:00
08:00
07:00
06:00
05:00
04:00
03:00
02:00
01:00

First Half

20:00

ARE YOU SENT?

The Messenger of the LORD appeared to Gideon and said, "The LORD is with you, brave man." Gideon responded, "Excuse me, sir! But if the LORD is with us, why has all this happened to us? Where are all the miracles our ancestors have told us about? Didn't they say, 'The LORD brought us out of Egypt?' But now the LORD has abandoned us and has handed us over to Midian." The LORD turned to him and said, "You will rescue Israel from Midian with the strength you have. I am sending you."

JUDGES 6:12-15, *(GOD'S WORD)*

Warm-Up
If God is sending you, then He will be your strength.

Game Time

I was doubtful, inadequate and unsure. These are just a few words that describe how I felt about becoming a coach. I had more reasons why I could *not* coach than I had reasons that I could. To be honest, I didn't think that I had what it took to do the job. Fear paralyzed me and threatened to keep me from reaching my full potential.

Gideon wrestled with fear too. The Messenger of the LORD (also called the Angel of the LORD) had called him to lead the Israelites into battle, and to save them from the oppressive hand of the mighty Midianites.[1] Gideon wanted to be faithful, but he felt inadequate for the task. So he let his reservations be known.

Interestingly, even though Gideon was dealing with a gamut of emotions, the Messenger of the LORD nonetheless told him that he was a "brave man" (Judges 6:12). Gideon must have done a double take. He knew himself better than anyone else, especially his weaknesses.

You know yourself better than anyone—both your strengths and your weaknesses. If you are like me, too often you will listen to your enemy as he reminds you of every mistake, shortcoming and human vulnerability. Too often you will believe him when he tells you that you are inadequate or even disqualified because of your faults. Yet those are lies that foment fear.

When fear knocks, you need to listen to the voice of the One who has called you instead of the deception from the one who wants to destroy you. It is not until you see past the doubts in front of you that you will realize the strength He has placed inside of you. He calls you simply to step up in the strength that He has supplied.

God wants to add His super to your natural, whereas Satan wants to overshadow and even take away your call. God's strength is made perfect in your weakness. The enemy only has power when he gets you to focus on your limitations so that he can undermine you.

When you trust in God, you become partners with Him! God and you become a power couple. You can move forward in faith, and the supernatural can take place as it did when Gideon led the Israelites against the Midianites.

A big question: Has God called you? Is He sending you? Is He telling you that you are brave? If the answer is yes, then He will be your strength and you have no reason to doubt or fear.

TIMEOUT

Read Psalm 27:1; Isaiah 41:10; John 14:1.

PRAYER TIME

Lord, help me to see myself the way You see me. By Your strength I am well able to accomplish that which You have set before me. I trust in Your plan for my life and I walk in confidence, knowing that You will give me the wisdom to execute Your life plan for me. Amen.

 **Clipboard Notes**

Note

1. In Evangelical Christianity, the Messenger of the LORD (or Angel of the Lord) is considered a preincarnate appearance of Christ.

First Half

19:00

OVERCOMING THE FEAR FACTOR

And the angel said unto her, Fear not, Mary: for thou hast found favor with God. And, behold, thou shalt conceive in thy womb, and bring forth a son, and shalt call his name Jesus. He shall be great.

LUKE 1:30-32 *(ASV)*

Warm-Up

When you walk with God, fear does not have to be a hindrance in your life.

Game Time

Mary was just a teenager when the angel Gabriel appeared to her with a startling message. God had hand-picked her to give birth to a child who would change the world. Such news would unnerve most young girls, especially if they like Mary were not married. Any word from an angel would startle me. Yet Mary had no fear. She had God's favor and was ready to step forward in faith.

Are you ready? You may not get a message from an angel, but God wants to speak to you about His plans for you. Most likely at least some aspects of these plans will seem improbable, even impossible, and perhaps daunting. That's when the fear factor tries to set in. First you are surprised. Then you tremble, and you might be tempted to run. But don't. As a believer you can expect to hear from God. You can also count on His favor.

When you have the favor of God, you have no reason to fear, because the foundation for your life has already been paved. Besides, God is good and so are His plans for you. So what's to fear?

When I decided to step out in faith to become a head basketball coach, one of the greatest hurdles I faced was overcoming my own fears. I had to remind myself that as a Christian, I am a bearer of God's image; and God is love, mercy and grace. He is also a God of favor. Therefore, fear should not be a factor. This was true for Mary. It is true for me. And it is true for you as a believer too. Your testimony should be, "God has not given me a spirit of fear, but one of power, love and a sound mind" (see 2 Timothy 1:7).

When God speaks, you are set to give birth to something great in your life. Don't allow fear to cause you to question what God has planned, but allow your faith to cause you to follow what God has placed in your heart.

Remember: With God, fear is not a factor—favor is!

T I M E O U T

Read Psalm 34:4; Isaiah 41:10; 1 John 4:18.

P R A Y E R   T I M E

Father, I know that You are with me, and I thank You for that! My desire is to always do what pleases You. Lord, I want You to conceive and birth something great in my life. Help me to see myself the way You do so that fear doesn't tarnish the view of me. I receive Your favor. May Your favor go before me, leveling every mountain and filling every valley so that I might stay on a smooth path always moving toward my destiny. Amen.

Clipboard Notes

First Half

18:00

WHY COACH?

*Then David knew that the LORD had established him as king over Israel and
had exalted his kingdom for the sake of His people Israel.*

2 SAMUEL 5:12 *(CSB)*

Warm-Up

God has established you as a leader for the sake of the people you lead.

Game Time

God loves people. His top priority is always their well-being. One
way He takes care of people is to raise up good leaders—kings (such
as David) and coaches (such as you) who will always have in mind
the best interests of the people whom they lead.

As a coach, you have been established for the sake of your team,
not for your own legacy. God created each of your players, so that
means they are His people. But He has entrusted you to nurture
each of them, day in and day out, whether they follow Him or not.
So, in effect, they are your people too.

It is easy to let practice sessions, game plans, phone calls, media
interviews and meetings consume your time and attention. Several
days can pass by without being in touch on a personal level with
the most important asset God has given you: your players. But
remember that God cares about people, and He cares about how
you care for the ones in your sphere of influence.

Just as you form a game plan to compete against your opponents
in the arena (or on the field), so too you should create a game plan to
daily nurture the lives of your players. Just as you show game clips to

teach your players how to improve on the court (or field), so too you should sow words of wisdom to train them how to become better people off the court (or field). When you invest time teaching them how to be better people, they also become better players—and they will reap the benefits long after the final buzzer has sounded. There is life beyond the game.

The legendary John Wooden won 10 national championships as the head men's basketball coach at UCLA. He once said, "What you are as a person is far more important than what you are as a basketball player." Yes, winning a game is important, but winning in life is more important.

Another big question: When you ask yourself, "Why am I coaching?" hopefully the answer will be, "For the sake of His people!"

TIMEOUT
Read Psalm 84:11; Psalm 101:6.

PRAYER TIME
Lord, thank You that You have counted me worthy to lead Your people. Help me to realize my purpose in You. Keep me ever conscious of the fact that I have a great responsibility to Your people that You have established me over. Help me to set my agenda aside so that I can invest in those You have entrusted to me. For the sake of Your people, give me wisdom and an understanding heart. Amen.

Clipboard Notes

_____

_____

_____

_____

_____

First Half

17:00

AT YOUR SERVICE

For even the Son of Man came not to be served but to serve others and to give his life as a ransom for many.

MATTHEW 20:28 *(NLT)*

Warm-Up

The greatest leaders humble themselves and serve others.

Game Time

One Sunday morning, I watched my pastor as he washed the feet of everyone in our congregation, including mine. I was humbled and inspired. He was following in the footsteps of Jesus, but I wondered how many pastors would dare to do this simple act of service.

Today, it seems that most leaders want to be exalted and fawned over rather than taking the position of a servant (see Philippians 2:6-7). Players and fans want to be pampered too. They say it is not about them, but too often in reality it is. Yet Jesus told His disciples that He had given them a model to follow. His pattern was quite the opposite of what we often see today. Jesus always served others, right to His very last breath. He served wine at a wedding, healed the blind, fed the hungry, gave hope to the hopeless, washed His disciples' feet, and made possible eternal life for every sinner—that is, everyone who will receive it.

As a coach, you have been placed in a position of authority. Now what will you do with it? Some leaders mistake authority for the right to dominate and exercise power over other people. Others rightly see it as a platform from which to serve.

What motivated Jesus to become nothing and take the position of a servant? Love. What motivates you?

TIMEOUT

Read John 13:12-15; Philippians 5:3-7;
1 Peter 5:2-4.

PRAYER TIME

Father, I cannot begin to fathom how Your Son, Jesus, was so eager and able to serve. He not only served His disciples and the people of His day, but He also serves everyone ever born, giving us the way to forgiveness, reconciliation with You and eternal life. Thank You. And now I ask, as I coach my team, enable me to follow the model of Jesus. Humble me and allow me to serve my players and everyone else in my life. Show me how to walk in humility, love others, and serve at all times. Amen.

Clipboard Notes

_____

_____

_____

_____

_____

First Half

16:00

WHAT IS IN A NAME?

I will praise the name of God with a song,
And will magnify Him with thanksgiving.
PSALM 69:30 *(NKJV)*

Warm-Up
Your name is not just a word. It carries meaning and expectation.

Game Time
Some names stand out, needing little or no explanation. When you hear Jackie Robinson, John Wooden, Billie Jean King or Jackie Joyner-Kersee, what do you think? How about Tim Tebow, Gabby Douglas, LeBron James or Mia Hamm?

Each of these names instantly evokes images and feelings. The name is not just a word. There is something more. Each one represents a passion, value, memory, gesture, great play, bad move, memorable speech or enduring symbol. Jackie Robinson broke the racial barrier in baseball. John Wooden exemplified winning with integrity. Gabby Douglas was the first African American to win an individual Olympic gold medal in gymnastics and was also unashamed of her faith! Tim Tebow . . . well, he does his Tebowing.

Names carry meaning and expectation. But none is more important or powerful than God's many names. God's names represent the various aspects of His nature. He is known as Jehovah Jireh (The Lord Our Provider), Jehovah Nisse (The Lord Our Banner), Jehovah Shalom (The Lord Our Peace), Jehovah Rohi (The Lord Our Shepherd), El Shaddai (The God Who Is Sufficient for the Needs of His People), and many others. God is all of these things, and more.

You are known as coach or assistant coach. This is your title, but it also becomes your name. As with any title or name, coach carries meaning and expectation, from others and yourself. This can be good because a name helps identify who you are. But you limit yourself if you become fixated on the title "coach," and forget that in the same way that God has many names describing His various roles, you also have many.

The actual coaching of your sport is only a fraction of what God has called you to be in the lives of your players—let alone what He has called you to be in your family, school and church. Through coaching, you not only lay out a strategy of X's and O's, but you also are to be a mentor, counselor, authority and mender. When you wear these various hats, you build relationships and trust.

A true statement: People don't care what you know until they know that you care. While a coach will care, that isn't inherent in the name "coach." But it is part of being a friend, another good name for a coach to wear. A player will not know that you care if he or she doesn't know you by any other name than coach.

TIMEOUT
Read Genesis 35:11; Exodus 17:15;
Matthew 1:21.

PRAYER TIME
Lord, help me to remember that I am not just called to be a *coach*.
Help me to see past X's and O's. Open my eyes and give me spiritual
insight so that I can see the needs of my players beyond the court.
Grant me a wise and understanding heart just as You gave to Your servant
Solomon. Grace and enable me to wear the many hats of all the other
names of what being a coach entails: mentor, counselor, authority,
mender and friend. In the name of Jesus. Amen.

Clipboard Notes

_____

_____

First Half

15:00

WHAT ARE YOU SAYING?

A word fitly spoken is like apples of gold in pictures of silver.

PROVERBS 25:11 *(KJV)*

Warm-Up

Your words have power!

Game Time

You possess the power to build up and to break down. The Bible says that this power lies in the tongue (see Proverbs 18:21). There is no in-between when it comes to your words—you either inspire life or conspire with death.

With the privilege of coaching comes great responsibility. God has placed His trust in you to be a steward of His players. This entails many things, starting with a conscious awareness of what you speak into their lives. By this, I simply mean that your words have an impact. Throughout the season, there will be times when you will become angry, frustrated, tired and even disappointed, but you must never allow your emotions to override your responsibility to use the right words at the right time.

Once words have been released from your mouth, they cannot be retrieved. They will forever make an imprint. Harsh words will chisel away at one's identity, whereas kind words will help to reinforce God-given identity. But kind words need to be authentic and from the heart, not insincere or smooth talk. People know the difference.

There will always be times when you will need to instruct, correct or discipline a player, but you will need to make sure to choose your words wisely. Most importantly, you must seek a proper balance between positive words and constructive criticism. This is called the *sandwich technique*. The bread represents the uplifting words you speak, and the meat represents the instruction, correction or discipline. So the flow should go like this: Start with positive feedback, then give constructive feedback, and finally end with more positive feedback. That's how you have a sandwich.

A wise thought: Always rely on God's guidance before you say a word. Be quick to listen and slow to speak!

TIMEOUT
Read James 1:19.

PRAYER TIME

Lord, help me to bridle my tongue, as my desire is to only speak words of life into my players' lives. There are times when I become frustrated, but in my anger help me to follow Your Word, which says to avoid sin. In the times when I have to give constructive criticism, orchestrate my thoughts so that my words will be fitly spoken, and let me glorify You in all that I say. Amen.

Clipboard Notes

_____

_____

_____

_____

_____

First Half
14:00

WHAT ARE YOU HEARING?

Did God really say, "You must not eat from any tree in the garden"?
GENESIS 3:1 *(NIV)*

Warm-Up
Many voices will compete for your attention, so it is vital that
you know how to listen to the right voice.

Game Time
Players, administrators, alumni, reporters and friends each have
opinions and advice, and some have agendas. Many suggestions
will sound appealing, even tempting. So how do you know when to
accept and when to reject what you hear? How do you know when
something is of God and when it is not?

One surefire way to know the truth is to go to the Word. Scripture is not only God's story but it is also the blueprint for your life.
The counsel and instruction found on its pages should govern your
every thought and move. Only as it comes alive will you be able to
live in a manner that is holy, pleasing and acceptable to Christ.

Sometimes the big idea someone presents is so alluring that
you will be tempted to bypass God's counsel and assume it will all
work out. My advice is simple: Don't take a shortcut.

A. W. Tozer warned, "Don't pick out only happy verses. It would
be shocking to go through some Bibles and see how we underline
only happy verses." He is right. You cannot randomly apply God's
Word or take it to heart only when it is convenient and comfortable.
The instant you begin to entertain thoughts that are contrary to the

truth is the moment you become susceptible to making bad choices. Look at Genesis 3:1 at the start of this reading. Those words were Satan's lie to Eve. She was tempted, she believed the deception, and every human since has suffered the consequences.

As a sinner, you are susceptible and in need of God's grace. That is why it is important that you continue to stay in God's Word and aim for what is right. You must allow God's Word to be the voice of truth that you hear at all times. As you receive His truth, you will know how to act.

A good word: In college athletics, the NCAA manual sets rules by which coaches must abide. Do some coaches live outside of these parameters? Sure. The media regularly reports myriad violations. But as a believer, you are to be holy and set apart. This means that you don't operate the way the world does. You may think that the ones who violate the rules are getting ahead, but you must put your trust in God and continue to do what is pleasing in His sight.

In the end, the person who violates the rules will lose and you will win, because you chose to listen to the voice of truth.

TIMEOUT
Read Mark 4:9; John 18:37.

PRAYER TIME

Father God, I thank You for the example set forth by Christ in living a life of truth. That same power that dwells in Christ to operate in integrity is in me because I choose to believe in and serve You. Jesus was tempted in every manner. Likewise, because of my humanness, I too shall be tempted to compromise. Lord, give me the grace to run this race, yet without sin.

I will choose to listen to Your voice of truth. Amen.

Clipboard Notes

_____

_____

_____

_____

First Half

13:00

THE COST OF MAKING AN ASSUMPTION

And then he told them, "Go into all the world and preach the Good News to everyone."

MARK 16:15 *(NLT)*

Warm-Up

One of the most important lessons you can learn is to never assume anything.

Game Time

Often, as a coach, you will make an assumption. You're busy with so many details, so it's natural and it's way too easy to do.

Assumptions come in so many ways. You will presume that your players know what to do in certain game situations, or that they have heard your instructions about a specific play and will follow them. You made it clear, but were they listening? Were they learning? Will they remember?

Making an assumption always comes with a cost. There have even been times when games have been lost because an assumption was made, either by a player or by a coach. Make too many assumptions and it can jeopardize a season.

As costly as losing a game is, consider how it would be even costlier if a soul were to be lost because a Christian assumed someone was saved. That's easy to do, especially in the South where everyone smiles and goes to church. There are lots of moral, upright people, but do they know God? You may have one of those "nice" kids on your team or at your school, but does he or she follow Jesus?

God has given us the Great Commission: "Go, therefore, and make disciples of all nations, baptizing them in the name of the Father and of the Son and of the Holy Spirit, teaching them to observe everything I have commanded you" (Matthew 28:19-20). Therefore it is the responsibility of every believer to lead others to Christ, even the nice kid on the team. Don't assume anything.

An important side note: If you happen to be reading this book and you have never received Christ as your personal Savior, now is the time! The only way to reach Father God is through His Son, Jesus Christ, who died on the cross for your sins. According to Romans 10:9, "If you confess with your mouth, 'Jesus is Lord,' and believe in your heart that God raised Him from the dead, you will be saved."

Salvation is for all who call upon the name of the Lord. It is simple. Just pray this prayer now (or use your own words):

Lord, as one who has not made the decision to follow You, I declare that now is the time. I ask that You forgive me for my sins and cleanse me from all unrighteousness. I confess that Jesus is Lord over my life, and I do believe that You raised Him from the dead. His resurrection gives me eternal life, and I thank You for that! Amen.

TIMEOUT
Read Ecclesiastes 10:13; John 8:32.

PRAYER TIME
Lord, as a believer, I choose to commit myself to Your Great Commission to make disciples of all nations. Give me a spirit of boldness to reach out to the lost, and give me a spirit of discernment to know who is in need of You. Amen.

 **Clipboard Notes**

_____

_____

_____

First Half
12:00

BACK IN BOUNDS

If we confess our sins, He is faithful and righteous to forgive us
our sins and to cleanse us from all unrighteousness.

1 JOHN 1:9

Warm-Up
No matter what you have done, Christ can forgive and restore you.

Game Time

Do you sometimes feel as if you are out of bounds with Christ? Perhaps you have fallen back into a life of sin that you thought you had left behind. Somehow old habits have crept back in and caused you to falter.

Well, the good news is that God is a God of second chances. His mercy endures forever. He wants you to get back into the game.

Of course Satan wants to bombard you with feelings of guilt, pushing you to the point of fearing that you can't come back to Christ. He will tell you that you have gone too far, that God will never forgive you, and that there is no hope. When peppered with such thoughts, just remember that Satan is the father of lies.

God never said that He would cleanse you from *some* unrighteousness—He said *all* unrighteousness! Therefore, no matter what you have done, God is willing and able to forgive you and restore you to the starting line-up.

You can get your life back in bounds!

Start by admitting the wrongs that you have done. Confession is good for the soul. It acknowledges the fact that you have missed the mark. It also disables the enemy because it unveils his lies.

Then, ask for God's forgiveness. He is a faithful God who is ready to cleanse and restore you. When God forgives you, He brings you back into union with Him and His Spirit, which lives inside you.

Of course, feelings of guilt and condemnation will try to creep back into your mind. The enemy will remind you about your past. When this happens, just remember God's Word: "So now there is no condemnation for those who belong to Christ" (Romans 8:1, *NLT*).

The blood of Christ cleanses you and makes you whole again. Your sins are thrown into the sea of forgetfulness to be remembered no more. If God does not want to remember, then why should you? I once heard this saying: "When Satan tries to remind you of your past, remind him of his future!"

A truth you can count on: You're back in bounds. You have a future and a hope that are secured in Christ!

TIMEOUT
Read John 3:16; Colossians 1:13-14.

PRAYER TIME

Dear Lord, I confess that I have fallen short. I have sinned and need Your forgiveness for my unrighteousness. I know that my only hope is in You. I want to return to You, my first love. I want to get back in the game, but I know that the only way to return is through Your forgiveness and a restoration of our relationship. Thank You for making me whole again. Amen.

Clipboard Notes

_____

_____

_____

_____

_____

First Half

11:00

A TRIPLE THREAT

Then David enquired of the LORD yet again. And the LORD answered him and said, Arise, go down to Keilah: for I will deliver the Philistines into thine hand. So David and his men went to Keilah.

1 SAMUEL 23:4-5 *(KJV)*

Warm-Up
You can be in position to hear from God and obey His direction.

Game Time
Good basketball players master what is called the triple threat. With knees bent, body weight shifted to the pivot foot, and both hands gripped on the ball, the player has options. From this position, she can pass, shoot or dribble—the triple threat!

A defender never knows which move the ball handler will make or if there will be a fake, so she has no idea how to defend. The low center of gravity of the triple threat makes it even more difficult for an opponent to knock a player off balance or throw her back on her heels.

This powerful triple-threat stance enables an offensive player to make a solid decision about whether she will pass, dribble or shoot.

In the spiritual realm, the triple-threat position is prayer. When praying, you can be in the presence of God, hear from Him and talk to Him. Your opponent the devil lurks about seeking whom he can devour, but his moves become futile in the face of prayer.

Moreover, whenever you face a big decision in life, you need to be in this spiritual stance. In prayer, you have all of God's options and His power to respond.

In 1 Samuel 23:4, David inquired of the Lord about going to battle because the Philistines were fighting against Keilah. When you pray to God, you should expect to hear from Him just as David heard from Him, but you also have to be prepared to respond.

David had prayed once and had received an answer from God, but the people were afraid and did not want to go to battle. So there was no response—no action. David prayed a second time and received the same message from God. This time David led his men into battle and saved the inhabitants of Keilah.

Prayer puts us in a position of power where Satan, our greatest opponent, will not be able to knock us off balance or put us back on our heels. Prayer moves us into the presence of God to receive His peace. Prayer puts us in a place where we can hear from God and receive His clear plan. Prayer prepares us to be obedient by responding to God's direction.

Some good advice: NFL coach Tony Dungy says, "For every high in life, I know there can be a low. I find my strength in prayer."[1]

TIMEOUT

Read Matthew 6:9-13; 1 Peter 3:12.

PRAYER TIME

Father, I thank You for Jesus, who died on the cross and who gives me access to the very throne of God through prayer and supplication. Always remind me to let prayer be my first priority when I am in need of direction.

Quiet my soul to hear from You so that I can receive Your direction, and give me the courage to respond to Your direction. In Jesus' name. Amen.

Clipboard Notes

Note

1. Tony Dungy, National Day of Prayer Promo, http://www.youtube.com/watch?v=N3CtQu_gnpM (accessed March 19, 2013)

First Half

10:00

ARE YOU PREPARED?

Be prepared in season and out of season; correct, rebuke and encourage—with great patience and careful instruction.

2 TIMOTHY 4:2 *(NIV)*

Warm-Up
Prior proper planning prevents poor performance.

Game Time

My collegiate coach was always ready to instill a new principle in the minds and hearts of her players. On many days, Sylvia Hatchell would select and share a quote or pithy phrase that, if applied, would improve the quality of our lives both on and off the court. I can still hear her wise words ringing loud and clear.

Coach Hatchell had some favorites. Every North Carolina player will remember her repeatedly saying, "Prior proper planning prevents poor performance." That is a lot of *P*'s! But it drives home the point.

A clever saying like this one gets your attention, but how do you begin to prepare? Being prepared involves a commitment *to something*. Let me explain.

Imagine that your team is in a tussle against your archrival. The opposing point guard hits a jump shot, putting her team up by two points with just two seconds remaining on the game clock. You have no timeouts left.

Is your team ready for the heat of this battle? Have they ever been in a close game? Have you taught them a play to score from full court? If so, your team can run the play with confidence. If not, they are not prepared.

While being prepared is no guarantee you will win the game, at least you have a shot. A lack of planning and instructing will likely result in confusion, and a last-second loss in our tight-game scenario.

The need to be prepared come game time is obvious in athletics. There is also a spiritual readiness that you need if you are to be an effective member of God's team. In Ephesians, this groundwork is called putting on the full armor of God.

The best way you can be prepared is by knowing and applying God's Word. For example, you may find yourself in a situation where you need to lead someone in a prayer of repentance or assist others in their walk with Christ. You won't always have a Bible handy, but if you have hidden His Word in your heart, you will be confident, equipped and ready to act.

A new fresh approach: See each Scripture as a play in God's playbook. Make every effort to memorize "plays" and you will be prepared to rebuke, correct and encourage with great patience and teaching.

TIMEOUT
Read Ephesians 6:10-24.

PRAYER TIME
Lord, grant me a strong desire to prepare myself through the reading of Your Word. Help me to memorize Your Word so that I can be prepared to share the gospel with others. Amen.

Clipboard Notes

_____

_____

_____

_____

_____

First Half

09:00

READY TO ASSIST

When Moses' hands grew heavy, they took a stone and put it under him, and he sat down on it. Then Aaron and Hur supported his hands, one on one side and one on the other so that his hands remained steady until the sun went down.

EXODUS 17:12 *(CSB)*

Warm-Up

A strong leader always has people who will watch his or her back.

Game Time

You have probably heard the story of Moses, Aaron and Hur. The Israelites were in an intense battle. Moses had instructed one of his assistants, Joshua, to select some men to fight against the Amalekites.

Moses took God's staff in his hand and went to a hilltop overlooking the battle. Now, this is the ideal situation for Satan to plant seeds of discord. I can hear the troops saying, "Moses wants us to go fight while he just stands on a hill and does nothing?"

Satan wants you to lose focus by mumbling and grumbling about the duties you've been given. When you lose focus, you do not succeed. And you do not grow.

The tougher the situation, the more likely you will improve in areas where you may have no experience. And responsibility prepares you to lead more effectively when the baton is passed and you become the one in charge.

Even though Moses stood on the hilltop while Joshua and his men were fighting, his role bore great significance. Each time he raised his hands, Israel prevailed over the Amalekites. Whenever his hands were down, the Amalekites advanced. Seeing the connection, Moses and his assistants were determined to keep Moses' arms lifted high. When Moses grew weary, Aaron stood on one side and Hur stood on the other side to assist him. They remained and persevered until the battle was won.

What a powerful moment! Imagine how Moses must have felt. It must have been comforting to know that his assistants had his back—or in this situation, his arms.

I can relate. Toward the end of the 2012-2013 season, I was traveling home with the Elon University women's basketball team after a road game. One of my players came to the front of the bus and simply told me, "We appreciate you." For me, her words were just as much support as Aaron and Hur's assistance was to Moses in the heat of battle. I melted.

A good idea: When you are the assistant, watch your leader's back, because someday you will need someone to watch yours.

TIMEOUT
Read Romans 16:2; Philippians 2:4;
Hebrews 13:17.

PRAYER TIME
Lord, when I am the assistant, give me an attitude of serving and obeying whomever You put in authority over me. Show me how to hold up his (her) arms just as Aaron and Hur held up the arms of Moses. And prepare my heart to lead when it is time. Then when I am the leader, surround me with Your people who will watch my back. Give me an appreciation for their assistance and let me always give You all of the glory, for ultimately You are the one who watches my back. Amen.

Clipboard Notes

_____

_____

_____

First Half

08:00

YOU CANNOT DO IT ALONE

You will certainly wear out both yourself and these people who are with you, because the task is too heavy for you. You can't do it alone.

EXODUS 18:18 *(CSB)*

Warm-Up

No matter how talented you are, you cannot do everything alone.

Game Time

Nike's slogan is *Just do it.* I have news for you: That is a great motivator, but as a coach, you can't do *it* alone. *It* is too big for one person.

This wise advice didn't come from Tom Landry or any other great sports figure; rather it was given to Moses by his father-in-law, Jethro. Moses needed the advice, because at that time, from morning until evening, he was sitting as a judge for the people of Israel. Jethro was downright blunt. He made it very clear that what Moses was doing was not good. He recommended that Moses appoint God-fearing and trustworthy men as officials to judge the people. The ones appointed would judge the minor cases, leaving the major cases for Moses. This would lighten Moses' load, lengthen his days of leadership, and prevent burnout.

This sounds like wise counsel from someone who cared.

Every leader must possess the ability to delegate responsibilities, or to find some way to lighten his load. To accomplish this, as a leader, you must make sure that you surround yourself with people you can trust. You must not only surround yourself with people you can trust, but you must also be open to their opinions. Moses was a good listener and was open to suggestions from others. This does not mean that you have to implement every idea given to you, but it is always good to seriously consider each one.

When the great coach, Tom Osborne, was named athletic director at the University of Nebraska, one of his first actions was to assemble the entire staff, from head coaches to locker-room attendants. He had each person list his or her ideas for improvement in the department, and then he implemented as many as possible, including one from a custodian.

If you don't listen and act, as Moses and Tom Osborne did, then you will not have the trust of your staff and team. In fact, the players will withhold good ideas if you come across as unapproachable.

You must also take the time to teach those whom you have gathered around you. They need to know your philosophy, way of thinking, and way of conducting business. Before Moses released the men he had appointed as leaders, he instructed them about God's statutes and laws so that they could judge accordingly. There has to be streamlined consistency flowing from the head leader down through all extensions.

Something to remember: Being a head coach is a great responsibility that can get heavy at times. But it is a responsibility that must be shared with others—both human assistants and God. It can't be done alone!

T I M E O U T
Read Exodus 18:21; Romans 12:4;
Ephesians 4:11-16.

P R A Y E R   T I M E
Lord, help me to make great disciples of the people who surround
me, so that I can release more responsibilities to them. This will help
reduce the heavy load that coaching can become. Give me ears to hear,
a heart that is open, and a strong discernment for ideas that will create a
more efficient and effective work environment. Amen.

Clipboard Notes

_____

_____

First Half

07:00

INSULTS AND BLESSINGS

*Be compassionate and humble, not paying back evil for evil
or insult for insult but, on the contrary, giving a blessing, since you
were called for this, so that you can inherit a blessing.*

1 PETER 3:8-9 *(CSB)*

Warm-Up

As a coach, someone will insult you. The question is not when will
it happen; rather, how will you respond?

Game Time

Coach, prepare yourself for insults, for they will surely come—and
they can come at the most unexpected times.

Recently, my younger brother and I were reliving moments of
my mother's life. As we exchanged stories, once again I was touched
by my mother's values and character. My brother told one story I
had never heard. He recounted a time when he and my mother
were traveling together by car. They encountered a man who was
disturbed by how she drove, and he proceeded to shout some
very obscene and derogatory words in her direction. How did she
respond? She said, "God bless you and have a nice day."

When I heard this story, I was proud of her and inspired. In the
flesh, it is too easy to lash out in retaliation, responding to an insult
with a bigger insult of our own. That doesn't work. It only frustrates
everyone, or worsens the situation. My mother wasn't offended by
the ugly words, nor was she insulted. Instead, she deflated the road
rage. She followed the Word of God, giving a blessing rather than
a curse.

As a coach, you are a public figure and therefore subject to the praises and insults of others. A fan may not like a play you called, a player you recruited, or the suit you wore. In America, our constitution guarantees freedom of speech, as it should. This allows for various opinions, even negative ones; but it doesn't assure respect or civility, both of which seem to be in short supply these days.

While you may need to be tough skinned, you can also see the insults thrown your way as opportunities to demonstrate God's love. You can even be a blessing to your adversaries.

Something to think about: Of course, some fans will sing your praises, even when you make a mistake. It is easier to bless people who are kind to you, but you need to be just as much of a blessing when the words are hurtful.

TIMEOUT

Read Proverbs 12:16; Luke 6:35.

PRAYER TIME

Lord, Your adversaries hurled insults at You, therefore I know that
I am not exempt from the same kind of treatment. Help me to always
operate in Your Spirit and be totally dependent on You to help me endure
the times when I am insulted. Christ gave the greatest example of this on
the cross when He said, "Forgive them for they know not what they do."
I desire to have the compassion and humility to be able to say
this and mean it on a daily basis. Amen.

Clipboard Notes

_____

_____

_____

_____

_____

First Half

06:00

GOD IS WITH YOU

The One who sent Me is with Me. He has not left Me alone,
because I always do what pleases Him.

JOHN 8:29 *(CSB)*

Warm-Up

God will never abandon you.

Game Time

You are where you are because God placed you there. It was ordained from the foundation of the Earth. God does not guide you to a place and then drop you off and say, "See you later." He sends you and then He stays by your side as long as you are seeking to please Him.

The doors that God opens in your life, no man can shut. The doors that God shuts, no man can open. You should always rest in the fact that because you have committed your ways to God, your steps are now ordered by the Lord. When you stand firm on this truth, you should have no reason to worry.

In this profession, with its demands and exalted expectations, job security can be questionable. Just like radio disc jockeys, coaches come and go, sometimes for good reasons and other times at the whim of an administration.

You should not worry about whether your employer is going to keep you in place or fire you—stressing over that is energy wasted. Just direct your focus on doing what God has called you to do. What good can you add to your life by worrying? Besides, God's people don't get fired, they just get redirected and shifted into another purpose for which God has called them. Every year you stay in your current post, you can rest knowing that God wants you there. When it is time to move on, you will discover how God has prepared you. When you submit to Him, all things work together for His good (see Romans 8:28).

You have the same promise that Solomon had. David urged his son to be strong and of good courage because God was with him (see 1 Chronicles 28:20). In the New Testament, James 4:8 includes the reminder that when you come near to God, He comes near to you—and since He is omnipresent, He is already quite close.

A comforting thought: Wherever you are, God is there too!

TIMEOUT

Read 1 Chronicles 28:20; Romans 8:28; James 4:8.

PRAYER TIME

Father, I know that You are with me, and I thank You for that! My desire is to always do what pleases You so that Your presence is with me. Amen.

Clipboard Notes

_____

_____

_____

_____

_____

First Half

05:00

LIGHT, CAMERA, ACTION

*Let your light shine before men, so that they may see your good works
and give glory to your Father in heaven.*

MATTHEW 5:16 *(CSB)*

Warm-Up
Let your light shine at all times.

Game Time

In every sport, there is practice and then there is the game. During practice, the atmosphere is more relaxed, but when the lights go on, the score counts.

If you have played or coached for very long, you will have come across athletes who play one way in practice and altogether another way in the game. Sometimes the athlete is lackadaisical during drills but puts on a game face and delivers when up against an opponent. Other times, a hard-driving, very skilled player outperforms everyone during workouts but then looks like a deer caught in the headlights when the game is played on the big stage.

In your Christian walk, it is always game time. The lights are always on. You are always on stage. The way you live your life should be a recruiting tool for Jesus. Your private life should be no different than your public life—meaning the way you practice should be the way you play when it counts. You should be a light that shines so that people will wonder why you illuminate so brightly. You can bring glory to God in heaven if you choose to be a light.

Here is a simple way to remember this concept:

- *Light.* You are called to be a light. You cannot be a light if you are walking in darkness.
- *Camera.* People are always watching to see if you are who you say you are.
- *Action.* You are called to be not only a hearer of God's Word but also a doer. You are called to walk in His ways at all times.

TIMEOUT

Read Isaiah 60:1; Joel 2:11; James 1:23.

PRAYER TIME

Lord, I thank You for Your example that You established in Your Son, Jesus Christ, who was the greatest light to ever live here on Earth. Fill me with Your Spirit so that I am able to be a light that shines before men for Your glory. Amen.

Clipboard Notes

_____

_____

_____

_____

_____

First Half

04:00

FOLLOW THROUGH ON YOUR PROMISES

I watch over My word to accomplish it.
JEREMIAH 1:12 *(CSB)*

Warm-Up

It is one thing to make a promise, and altogether another thing to follow through on that promise.

Game Time

God is faithful to His word. He watches over it to make sure that it achieves that which He said it would. When He speaks, He also follows through. When God says something, you can count on it. His word will never return to Him void. The task at hand will be accomplished.

For a basketball player, follow through can be the perfected finishing touch of a shot that sees nothing but net. For a baseball pitcher, sound follow through finishes off a great pitch and helps the player to stay injury free. For a quarterback, proper follow through increases the precision of each pass he throws.

God is a God of follow through. In sports, coaches preach follow through. But when it comes to the pledges you make to others and to God, do you follow through? Or is follow through something you only wish would happen someday?

When it comes to the words you speak, follow through is finishing that which you have promised to do. What does your word mean? When you say something, do you act on it? Are you faithful to your word? I know, this is tough medicine, but I ask myself the same questions because being a keeper of my word means everything.

Following through on what you promise to do gives your words credibility and validation. When you give someone your word, you are asking them to give you their trust. So what you do after you speak says a lot about you. Of course, you will come short sometimes—everyone does. That is where forgiveness comes in. But just because a promise has been broken doesn't mean that you don't make another one, and find a way to keep it!

God wants you to put your trust in Him. He asks that you trust in Him with your whole heart and lean not to your own understanding. Trust is essential in any relationship. Not following through in both word *and* deed damages trust, and it can jeopardize the very foundation of a relationship.

A promise to count on: Your word is one of the most important possessions you have. Preserve it by being one who watches over your word to accomplish it. Be known as a person who follows through.

TIMEOUT

Read Psalm 119:2; 2 Corinthians 1:20;
1 John 2:5.

PRAYER TIME

Dear Lord, thank You for Your word. You always follow through on Your promises. I know that I can always trust You and count on You. I want to follow Your example. I want my word to always mean something. Help me to follow through on whatever I say, so that people will trust me and see You. Let me watch over my thoughts and the words that come out of my mouth. Let them always give You glory. Amen.

 Clipboard Notes

_____

_____

_____

First Half

03:00

BE CHRISTLIKE

*Therefore, be imitators of God, as dearly loved children.
And walk in love, as the Messiah also loved us and gave Himself for us,
a sacrificial and fragrant offering to God.*

EPHESIANS 5:1-2 *(CSB)*

Warm-Up

Being an imitator of Christ requires sacrifice.

Game Time

When I was younger, my favorite NBA player—besides my uncle, David Thompson—was Michael Jordan. I wanted to be like Mike!

Michael, or MJ as we called him, played for the Chicago Bulls. His teams won 6 NBA titles and he led the league in scoring 10 times. His playmaking was the stuff that every basketball player dreams about and that legends are made off.

Glued to my television set every time the Bulls played, I watched Michael's every move. I noticed not only his dribbling, passing and shooting, but also his work ethic, attitude and passion. I was impressed, and I determined that when I played, I was going to wear the same number 23 as he did—*so I could be like Mike.*

My MJ likeness didn't stop there. I desperately wanted a pair of Air Jordans—the shoes named after him—but my family couldn't afford the hefty price tag. Luckily I had a connection with someone who worked at a shoe store and was given a pair. They were a size too small and really hurt my feet, but I didn't care because I wanted to be an imitator of Michael. I was willing to sacrifice comfort to be like my hero.

Being like Mike was not just about wearing the number 23; it also extended to replicating the level of determination, work ethic, commitment and sacrifice that made him the best in the game. He even practiced hard. If I was going to excel like Mike, I needed to work like Mike too. I needed to adopt his positive character traits.

I played college basketball at the University of North Carolina, Michael Jordan's alma mater. We won a lot of games, and the school made a poster of me dunking "Jumpman" style *like Mike*. I even hit a winning shot in the national championship game—*just like Mike*.

I had fun emulating Michael Jordan, and his inspiration certainly made me a better basketball player. But in life, my greatest desire is to be like Christ. Just as I wanted to play in Michael's shoes, I have a greater desire to walk in God's commands, promises and plans.

Christ is my model, hero and Lord. He is mercy, grace, hope, justice, love, peace, truth, forbearance, eternal life, and so much more. As I seek to be like Christ, I see myself taking on and growing in these traits.

What about you? Whom do you want to imitate? Whose shoes do you want to wear? Here is an even tougher question: Are you wearing God's name on a T-shirt only (or thinking about Him on Sunday mornings only), or is He living in your heart and evident in your life every day?

Being an imitator of Christ requires sacrifice, but the reward is eternal. I was willing to sacrifice the comfort of my feet in wearing shoes that were way too small so that I could be an imitator of Mike for something as temporal as a basketball game. How much more should I be willing to sacrifice to be like Christ? How about you?

A big question: Are you willing to do whatever it takes to be Christlike?

TIMEOUT
Read 1 Corinthians 4:16; 1 Corinthians 11:1; Philippians 2:1-11.

PRAYER TIME

Lord, I desire to be more like You. Please align my heart with Yours so that I know what I need to sacrifice of myself. The Messiah gave all of Himself as a sacrifice for me, so now I want to give all of myself as a sacrifice to Him so that I can be more like Him. Amen.

Clipboard Notes

_____

_____

_____

_____

_____

First Half

02:00

YOU ARE CAPABLE

But Caleb quieted the people before Moses and said, "Let us go up
at once and occupy it, for we are well able to overcome it."
NUMBERS 13:30 *(ESV)*

Warm-Up
Sometimes you are the one who keeps you from doing
all that you are able to do.

Game Time
I like the word "capable." A person who is capable has the attributes required for performance or accomplishment. As a coach, I want capable players on my team—ladies who can both perform on the court and accomplish much in their lives beyond basketball.

What is it that often keeps players (and others) from performing and accomplishing much? Division. A team (or kingdom) divided against itself cannot stand (see Mark 3:24). A person can even be divided against herself, especially when she doubts her ability to perform or accomplish a task.

To see how doubt can sabotage a person, dissect in half the word "capable." Picture it as "cap" and "able." When you doubt, you put a cap on what you are able to do! *Doubt always divides.*

Look at the Israelites (see Numbers 13:30). They were divided, even though they were able. Of the twelve leaders, just two believed that they could overtake the so-called giants who occupied the land that God had promised them. Caleb was one who believed and declared that they were able—he knew that God was with them. The naysayers were doubtful. They capped their ability, and thus saw themselves as having no chance to succeed.

You know God's plans for you and His ability to deliver. Yet doubt always creeps in. You become what James 1:8 calls a double-minded man who is "unstable in all his ways." Another translation reads, "A person who has doubts is thinking about two different things at the same time and can't make up his mind about anything" (*GOD'S WORD*).

I already admitted that I had fears about becoming a head coach. I struggled with doubt for quite some time. Yes, I was capping my God-given ability. In fact, I was capping what God wanted to do that would exceed my human ability.

What made me decide to step out in faith? I did as Caleb did. He silenced the naysayers; I silenced the voice of doubt. He spoke to the people with a voice of truth and affirmation, saying, "We are able to overcome"; I spoke to myself with a voice of truth and affirmation, saying, "I am capable and more than able to get the job done."

The thoughts that you allow to occupy your mind will determine whether you will overcome or be overwhelmed by your circumstances. Don't let your doubts put a *cap* on what you are *able* to do.

A truth and affirmation worth believing: You are capable! You are more than able to do that which God is calling you to do. God always equips those whom He calls, so you can silence all negative thinking and know that you are well able to overcome any fear or doubt. You can walk into your promised land that awaits you.

TIMEOUT
Read 1 Samuel 7:3; Mark 9:23; John 14:12.

PRAYER TIME
Lord, help me to stand on Your Word, which confirms that I am capable. In Philippians 4:13, it says, "I am able to do all things through Him who strengthens me." I ask that You strengthen me and give me the courage to walk in Your purpose and plan for my life. Help me to have a stable and undivided mind by keeping my focus on You and my trust in You. Amen.

Clipboard Notes

_____

_____

_____

_____

_____

First Half

01:00

A SEASON OF REFRESHING

*But the news about Him spread even more, and large crowds
would come together to hear Him and to be healed of their sicknesses.
Yet He often withdrew to deserted places and prayed.*

LUKE 5:15-16 *(CSB)*

Warm-Up

You need to discover how to maintain a balance between
taking care of others and taking care of yourself.

Game Time

Jesus has a big heart for people. Operating out of compassion, He
often reached out to meet the needs of those who surrounded Him.
But He also took time to withdraw from the crowds, allowing
Himself seasons of refreshing.

Jesus' model is one to follow.

You can only pour out so much of yourself before you need to
be refilled. You will find a proper balance only when you make sure
that you take care of yourself in the process of taking care of others.

Coaching is about balance as well. You will always have many
things pulling you in opposite directions at the same time. You
have to meet the needs of your players, staff, administration, fans,
community, media and family. Oh, and then there are your needs
too. Pull, tug, stretch, push, go the extra mile, go the extra 10 miles,
have faith, take a deep breath, and start the cycle all over again.

You can only give out what you have inside. If you find yourself
on a treadmill or feeling burnt out, then you will not have much

to give out. A season of refreshing will look different for each person. Maybe it is taking a few minutes to drink coffee and read the psalms. For you it could be going for a drive in the country and listening to some worship music. For some, it may be getting away from everything for a few days to be alone with God.

A big hint: Make seasons for refreshing part of your routine, then you will always have something to give from inside and will be less likely to ever face burnout.

TIMEOUT
Read Psalm 23:2; Psalm 107:29-31.

PRAYER TIME
Lord, there are so many needs and demands all around. I want to meet them all, but I know that I cannot do so in my own strength. I need You. And I need seasons of refreshing. Show me how to follow Your Son's example of withdrawing from the crowds to spend quiet time listening to Your voice and becoming refreshed. Amen.

Clipboard Notes

_____

_____

_____

_____

_____

The Clock Has Expired

00:00

IT'S HALFTIME!

Halftime is always a good time to reflect on how your team has played and an opportunity to revise your game plan if necessary.

QUESTIONS TO PONDER

What does your life look like?

What can it look like?

What changes can you implement to make this happen?

20:00

19:00

18:00

17:00

16:00

15:00

14:00

13:00

SECOND HALF

12:00

11:00

10:00

09:00

08:00

07:00

06:00

05:00

04:00

03:00

02:00

01:00

Second Half

🕑 20:00

A FRESH START

Therefore, if anyone is in Christ, he is a new creation.
The old has passed away; behold, the new has come.

2 CORINTHIANS 5:17 *(ESV)*

Warm-Up

No matter how poor your performance in the first half,
you will have another chance.

Game Time

Have you ever entered the locker room at halftime wishing that the first 20 minutes of the game hadn't happened? Wanting to press the delete key? Ready to start over?

Of course you have. Every coach has games that don't start well. Maybe your players were sluggish or out of sync. Perhaps every adjustment you made just made things worse. Sometimes a player on the other team is simply having a career game, and your team cannot stop her. What do you say to your players at halftime? (Or between innings in softball?)

I can still hear my college coach, Sylvia Hatchell, saying, "OK, that half is over. It's a new half and the score is zero to zero." She was cleaning the slate. The old things had passed away and the new were waiting. We needed to seize what was before us and not be derailed by what was behind us. (In track, you may have to wait until the next heat or competition, but there is always a next time.)

When you experience moments such as these, it's a good tactic to look forward. That's all you have. You cannot change the outcome of the first half, but you can learn from your mistakes, try not to repeat them, and play a better second half.

The same is true in life outside the arena (or stadium or pool). Sometimes you get off to a bad start or into a bad situation, whether it be in a relationship or a choice you have made. You can find yourself behind or facing impossible odds. The prodigal son did just that when he went astray. It was his own fault.

What do you do? If you are like most people, instead of starting over, you dig deeper into the pit of despair. By the time you realize there is a shovel in your hands and look up, you can't see daylight. The prodigal son ended up rooming with a bunch of hogs—literally!

No matter how deep the hole you're in or how far behind you are, you are never outside the reach of God. He can easily reach right down into that pit, pull you out, dust you off, and give you a fresh start in life. Sometimes all you need is a simple devotional reading such as this one to help you look up and grasp His hand.

The prodigal son realized his mistake before it was too late. He returned to his earthly father, who was ready and willing to give him a fresh start, a new half.

A truth worth writing down: Your heavenly Father is waiting to give you a fresh start. The things of the past are old and done. Behold the new has come.

TIMEOUT
Read Luke 15:11-32; John 3:3-8.

PRAYER TIME
Lord, I thank You for Your forgiveness, which allows me to
have a clean slate and a fresh start. I am grateful that You are faithful
and that Your mercies begin afresh each morning. Amen.

Clipboard Notes

_____

_____

_____

Second Half
19:00

WHERE ARE YOU?

The LORD said to Abram, after Lot had separated from him, "Now lift up your eyes and look from the place where you are, northward and southward and eastward and westward; for all the land which you see, I will give it to you."
GENESIS 13:14-15 *(NASB)*

Warm-Up
God's promises are bigger than your problems.

Game Time
God told Abram to travel to a faraway land. He was to leave behind his relatives and father's house. God made a promise and would eventually show Abram his destination, but not at first. In this new land Abram would be blessed. A great nation would be established, his name would be known, and he would be a blessing to many generations.

Abram departed as God had instructed. When he arrived at Canaan, God told him, "To your descendants I will give this land." Abram pitched his tent, built an altar, and called upon the name of the Lord.

No sooner than Abram had settled in, a famine swept through the place. This no doubt made Abram question everything he thought God had said. He was supposed to be blessed, his name great and his legacy grand. But there was no food. Had there been wax in his ears? Had he really heard from God?

Have you ever taken a step out in faith, maybe even taken a big risk, only to find yourself questioning your decision? Maybe you accepted a new job, moved to another state, or were given a big responsibility at church. You were excited and hopeful, but then the new situation took a turn for the worse. You started to wonder, *What in the world did I get myself into? This is not looking like all it was cracked up to be. God, You called me to leave for this?!*

I can identify with Abram. Change is uncomfortable in and of itself, but to take a risk thinking that you are obeying God and then have it end up looking and feeling like you are stepping backward is another story.

God told a deflated Abram, "Look from the place where you are, for all that you see I will give to you." God did not say to look *at* the place where you are, but to look *from* the place where you are toward the place you are going to be!

No matter your situation, you cannot afford to look at present circumstances. You must see beyond to the fulfillment of God's promise to you. Keep your eyes on the prize. Look *from* the place of disappointment, discouragement, hurt, unbelief, abandonment or brokenness and *believe* that what God has promised lies ahead.

It's a matter of trust. Where are you? Where are your thoughts? Are they on the problem or on the promise? Are you trusting God to come through for you? God's promises are bigger than your problems. All you need to do is trust God's way. He is faithful.

TIMEOUT
Read Psalm 59:9; Romans 4:20;
Galatians 4:28.

PRAYER TIME
Lord, I thank You that Your promises are true. Help me to keep my eyes lifted toward You, for You are where all my help comes from! Amen.

 **Clipboard Notes**

_____

_____

_____

Second Half
18:00

SPIRITUAL FITNESS

Bodily fitness has a certain value, but spiritual fitness is essential both for this present life and for the life to come.
1 TIMOTHY 4:8 *(PHILLIPS)*

Warm-Up
Spiritual fitness requires that you commit yourself to a spiritual work-out routine.

Game Time
At the beginning of each season you want to have the confidence that your team will contend for the conference title or at least do better than you did the previous season. For this to happen, you need to get off to a good start. To get off to a good start, you need all of your players to come back from the off season in top physical form. That doesn't always happen.

Have you ever noticed how God can take something from one context and apply it to another?

Early one season, some friends brought to my attention that my level of fitness was not all that great either. But my friends were not talking about my physical condition. They were concerned that I was out of shape spiritually. My spiritual endurance was fading—a reality made evident by my inability to focus on spiritual things for an extended period of time. I was winded and in need of a spiritual overhaul.

Why? Because I had fallen out of my routine of waking up and starting my day by praying and reading my Bible. I would put my time with God off in hopes of doing it later—and then would find myself giving Him the dregs at the end of the day. I was struggling to do the things I knew He was calling me to do and that I was capable of doing, including writing this book. In the midst of this struggle, God posed a very good question to me: *How are you going to write a book that emphasizes prayer if your own prayer life is practically nonexistent?*

Somewhere along the way, I had fallen off the wagon. I had allowed myself to become consumed with life's demands, and I had ended up feeling totally overwhelmed and spiritually dry. Even though I knew better, I had pulled away from the very thing that would sustain me: the disciplines that would give me the endurance to run the race called life.

So what did I do? I surrendered to my fitness coach, Jesus, in hopes of getting back on track. I asked God to redirect my focus—so that I could finish this book, but even more so that I could relieve my spiritual coach of being frustrated with me for not reaching my full spiritual potential.

How about you? Where are you in your level of spiritual fitness today?

TIMEOUT

Read Isaiah 40:28-31; 1 Corinthians 9:24-27; Hebrews 12:1-13.

PRAYER TIME

Lord, please forgive me for taking You for granted. Your Son died on the cross for me, which gives me direct access to You through my prayer life. Give me a hunger and a thirst for You that can only be quenched by You. Help me to stay focused on the things that are most important to You, so that I remain in great spiritual shape for Your glory and the advancement of Your kingdom! Amen.

Clipboard Notes

_____

_____

_____

Second Half
17:00

IT IS WRITTEN

*Stay awake and pray, so that you won't enter into temptation.
The spirit is willing, but the flesh is weak.*

MATTHEW 26:41 *(CSB)*

Warm-Up

God who is in you is greater than any temptation or
trouble you can ever encounter.

Game Time

When coaches develop their game plan, one of their main objectives
is to find the opponent's weaknesses. Once they recognize where the
other team is vulnerable, they can devise ways to exploit those weaknesses in the game.

Satan takes this same strategic approach when he comes to
upend your life. He wants to find out which buttons to push to
expose and exploit your weaknesses.

Jesus was led by the Spirit into the wilderness, where He fasted
for 40 days and 40 nights (see Matthew 4:1-3). It is no surprise,
having been without food for that long, that Jesus was hungry.
Perceiving Jesus' lack of nourishment as a possible weakness, Satan staged an attack.

He approached Jesus, questioned His relationship with God,
and asked Him to turn stones to bread. Satan kept hammering
away at the Messiah, attacking Him two more times (see Matthew 4:5-11). But Jesus was on His game, as He always is. He was

consistent in every way and resisted. What appeared to Satan as a weakness in Jesus actually was an opportunity for Jesus to humbly show His strength.

Coaches know the correlation between success and being consistent. You want to bring consistent defense and intensity to your game. You want scorers to be consistent night in and night out.

Jesus is our model. Without even a sliver of compromise, every time Satan attacked, Jesus was consistent in His response. He would simply say, "It is written" (Matthew 4:4).

Remember the power in the Word is the power that overcomes! Every time you are tempted to succumb and you weaken defensively, you can counterattack with the Word of God, which never fails. This is one reason why it is imperative for you to meditate on the Word daily as it makes deposits in your spirit. God's Word is what sustains and strengthens you.

TIMEOUT
Read Matthew 4:1-11; 1 John 5:5.

PRAYER TIME
Lord, I will commit myself to the reading of Your Word, as it sustains me from being weak. When temptation comes, empower me with Your Word. Let me simply and humbly say, "It is written." And may the glory of overcoming temptation be to You. Amen.

Clipboard Notes

_____

_____

_____

_____

_____

Second Half

16:00

EYES ON THE TARGET

Jumping out of the boat, Peter walked on the water to Jesus.
But when he looked down at the waves churning beneath his feet,
he lost his nerve and started to sink. He cried, "Master, save me!"

MATTHEW 14:29-30 *(THE MESSAGE)*

Warm-Up

When you fix your eyes on Jesus, your faith is perfected
and you are able to reach the goal He has set for you.

Game Time

One of the oldest acrostics in basketball is B.E.E.F. The "B" is for
"balance." The first "E" is for "eyes on target." The second "E" is for
"elbow straight." And the "F" is for "follow through." Each one is
important, but plenty of shots go into the basket even though the
shooter is off balance, has bent elbows or doesn't follow through.
But seldom will a ball find the hoop if the shooter's eyes aren't fixed
on the target. Each player in each sport has his or her own target.
A pitcher in baseball must get the ball over the plate. A swimmer
needs to reach the other end of the pool. A pole vaulter has to clear
the crossbar.

As important as sports goals are, at the heart of every great com-
petitor, both in the game and in life, is the discipline of focusing on
a greater purpose. Just look at what eyes taken off the target pro-
duced in the life of one of the disciples: Peter wanted to walk on water with Jesus. He was just fine until he shifted his eyes from Jesus to

the fierce, wind-driven waves. He became fearful and began to sink. I had that sinking feeling a few years back, when my dad was given only a few months to live. I was overcome by grief. As I was crying, the Holy Spirit gently reminded me to keep my eyes on God. I was overwhelmed by His peace and the knowledge that no matter the tumult around me, all was well with my soul.

What can you learn from Peter? No matter the final score, injury or pressure, when we keep our eyes on the target, all will be well with our souls, both in the game and in life.

TIMEOUT

Read 1 Corinthians 11:1; Hebrews 12:2.

PRAYER TIME

Lord, every time I take my eyes off of You, I'm like the disciple Peter; I sink into a sea of despair. Sometimes circumstances overwhelm me to the point of not knowing You're there. The pressure is mounting and the water is rising to my knees. I'm trembling from the fear of all my unfulfilled needs. But just when I am drowning in my failure to believe, You stretch out Your hand and offer Your grace to me. I have to keep my eyes on You, the One who gives me sight. Keep me grounded in my faith; remind me it's alright. Lord, help me to keep my eyes lifted to the hills from where all my help comes. Help me to keep my eyes on You so that my faith will not waver. Amen.

Clipboard Notes

_____

_____

_____

_____

_____

Second Half
15:00

REMAIN UNSHAKABLE

And David was greatly distressed; for the people spake of stoning him,
because the soul of all the people was grieved, every man for his sons and
for his daughters: but David encouraged himself in the LORD his God.

1 SAMUEL 30:6 *(KJV)*

Warm-Up
You can be strong under pressure when your strength comes from God.

Game Time
It was the opening game of the season, and so much excitement was in the air. The first home exhibition game marked my first as a head coach. As the game progressed, hecklers shouted, "Get your line up right! Get some offense in the game!" Sadly, these criticisms came from those who were supposed to be cheering us on. It's amazing how people may not physically stone you, but stone you with their very words.

But just as David did, I encouraged myself in the Lord. I prayed, *God, be a hedge of protection all around me; be my shield; be an unbreakable force field that surrounds me. Hide me under the shadow of Your wings!*

Know this: If God is for you, who in this whole world can be against you? Don't you dare be moved by what you see or hear. Remain unshakable! Leadership demands inner strength to carry the mantle of responsibility and not be unnerved.

You cannot control what goes wrong. Your best player might go down. The airplane might be delayed and cause you to be late for the finals. The media might call you the underdog. A player might transfer schools. When you feel upside-down, the real question is not "What am I going to do?" but "Who am I?"

Who am I really? Athlete? Coach? Winner? Champion? Those names only scratch the surface of who I am. Underneath it all, I am His. I give my all. I work, sweat and strain to be the very best. I perfect my craft by scouring old game videos. I recruit and develop good players. I strategize. I talk to mentors. But at season's end, wins and losses will not define my identity.

Good leaders have a firm trust and reliance that their worth comes from their position in Christ.

David was distressed and "encouraged himself in the LORD." What does that mean for coaches today? I come to Him before the stresses of the day in prayer and read the Bible for guidance. During a new crisis, my spirit cries, "God, help me!" Afterwards I remember to thank Him for His help and wisdom, alone and with a community of believers at my local church.

God longs to restore and refresh you. He wants to give you rest from the cares of this world so that when all is shaking on the outside, He is transforming you on the inside with His peace.

Remain unshakable in your faith, in your call, and in your relationship with Christ, no matter the circumstances

.

TIMEOUT
Read 2 Chronicles 20:12; Psalm 46:1-3;
2 Corinthians 1:8-10.

PRAYER TIME
Almighty God, thank You for being my Rock and my Shield. Thank You that Your kingdom is unshakable, and for the peace and wisdom I gain from being in Your presence. Please continue to refine me through the victories and defeats in my life. Help me to trust that my strength comes from You whether all is well or the world seems against me. Help me to remember that without You I can do nothing. In Christ's name. Amen.

 Clipboard Notes

_____

_____

Second Half

14:00

RIDING THROUGH THE STORM

Suddenly, a violent storm arose on the sea, so that the boat was being swamped by the waves. But He was sleeping.

MATTHEW 8:24 *(CSB)*

Warm-Up

If Jesus is in our boat, we can have peace in the midst of life's storms.

Game Time

One of my most memorable seasons in the WNBA was the 2001 season. We lost 10 of our first 11 games. But after that we lost only 4 games, finishing with an 18-14 record. Even though we barely qualified for the playoffs, all the other teams knew that we were a talented team on the verge of pulling things together. We stormed through the playoffs, beating the number-one and number-two seeds to win the Eastern Conference finals. For the first time in franchise history, we found ourselves in the WNBA finals. We eventually lost the WNBA championship to the L.A. Sparks, but it was a great ride, and I was able to witness something that would shape my way of thinking for the rest of my life.

I had always admired the spirit of my head coach, Ann Donovan. She was very direct, focused and composed. But our early-season struggles in 2001 gave me a whole new respect for her. Losing 10 games is a tough experience—in the life of a coach, it would be considered a pretty major storm. Now, Coach Donovan may have been pulling all of her hair out at home as our record got worse and worse, but she never displayed being rattled, and that shaped the belief system of her players and the way we responded as team-mates towards one another.

Our coach never placed blame, so we never pointed fingers at one another. She continued to encourage us, so we continued to encourage one another. After each loss, we would look at the re-mainder of our schedule and say, "We still have a chance to be . . ." There was a peace that sustained us through the storm. It would have been easy to cave in and give up, but the peace and calm our leader displayed assured us that somehow everything was going to be okay.

We all have to face storms in our lives. Many of these storms will be far greater than losing basketball games, but we must face them just the same. When the violent storm arose on the sea, the disciples came and woke Jesus up, because they were in a panic and thought they were going to die. Jesus asked them, "Why are you fearful, you of little faith?" (Matthew 8:26). Jesus then rebuked the winds, and calm was restored. We can follow His example by find-ing rest in the midst of our trials, having peace even as the winds howl around us, and believing that God is in control and will bring us through every storm and struggle we face.

TIMEOUT
Read Psalm 40:1-3; Isaiah 43:1-2;
Acts 27:14-25.

PRAYER TIME
Lord, I thank You that You have made available to me Your peace that surpasses all understanding. Help me to trust You, even when I am in the midst of a terrible storm, and to believe that You will bring me through it. Amen.

 **Clipboard Notes**

_____

_____

Second Half
13:00

REBOUNDING

*And the L*ORD* restored the fortunes of Job, when he had prayed for his friends. And the L*ORD* gave Job twice as much as he had before.*

JOB 42:10 *(ESV)*

Warm-Up
You serve a loving, forgiving and redeeming God.

Game Time
Players need to shoot and rebound the ball in order to gain points in a basketball game. When the ball drops through the net, the player scores, but when the shot misses, the ball can spring back or be rebounded. Offensive rebounding re-establishes or restores the opportunity to shoot, to score and to win.

Rebounding is a fundamental part of the game of basketball. Similarly, when the Christian "misses shots" or sins, God provides an opportunity to rebound from sin through His love and grace. You may have thought that you would never get over that one-point loss to your top rival—until you realized that loss pales in comparison to so many other things you could lose. In this life we will all encounter major losses, whether it be unemployment, a business loss, or the passing of a loved one. I have had my share of losses, so I can attest to the Scripture that states, "Many are the afflictions of the righteous, but the LORD delivers him out of them all" (Psalm 34:19, *NKJV*).

These types of losses cause such afflictions through which deliverance can only come from Christ. Too many times people try to use worldly means to anesthetize the pain, which serves as a temporary fix but only ends up leading us down a blind alley. If we finally release ourselves from the dead-end solutions, Christ can usher us right back to the God who heals us from all our brokenness and furnishes us with beauty for ashes.

There were times when the pain in my life was so intense, as I experienced the loss of my father, my marriage and my WNBA career all in a matter of weeks, that I thought I was going to cave in. So what do you do in those moments?

My inspiration came as I examined the life of Job. When Job lost all his children and possessions, he tore off his robe, shaved his head, and did the most important thing any of us can do in a time of loss: Job fell to the ground and worshiped his Maker.

Is this difficult to do? My experience has taught me that feelings do not always align with actions. I can remember being so depressed yet pressing through my pain to get to my praise. I did not *feel* like praising, and I did not *feel* anything while I was praising, but I continued in faith, knowing that God would honor my heart. That time reflected a climb from the pitfall of grief, and continuous worship sustained me.

A key to your ability to come back: In order to rebound from a loss, praise and worship to God are essential, no matter how you feel. When you place God higher than your circumstances, He honors this and blesses you, most importantly in your restored covenant with Him.

TIMEOUT

Read Psalm 26:11; 1 John 1:9; Luke 15:11-23.

PRAYER TIME

Loving Father, let me be reminded of the restitution cited in King David's song: "Those who sow in tears will reap harvest in glad song." Thank You for Your abounding grace, mercy and love that restore me when I miss and sin. Thank You that Your desire for me is to be humble and repentant, and to then get right back into the game. Thank You that You are the God who heals. I desire to pray for others while I continue to praise and worship You.

I am grateful for Your gift of forgiveness and eternal salvation through Your Son, Jesus Christ. In His name I pray. Amen.

CHARLOTTE D. SMITH

Clipboard Notes

_____

_____

_____

_____

_____

Second Half

12:00

HIDDEN POTENTIAL

So they inquired again of the LORD, "Is there a man still to come?" and the LORD said, "Behold, he has hidden himself among the baggage."

1 SAMUEL 10:22 *(ESV)*

Warm-Up

God inspires and equips those He calls to leadership.

Game Time

HGTV airs an intriguing television series, called *Hidden Potential,* where homebuyers view three different houses that need renovations or even an overhaul to build up the house for purchase. As the buyer conducts a guided tour, the project specialist illustrates computer-generated graphics that unveil the home's prospects. In some ways perhaps you are like this, as you need a design expert to reveal your hidden potential. That design expert is Jesus Christ. Your view of personal potential is oftentimes distorted and you cannot visualize your possibilities. This was the case with Saul when God decided to anoint him king over Israel.

Saul would be the next king, as God had called and anointed him, yet he could not see the potential in himself. When God calls you to something, God will equip you and inspire you through the Holy Spirit to do that very thing. When it was time for Saul to be presented as king before the people, they looked for him but could not find him, because he had hidden himself among the baggage. Just as Saul was hidden potential amongst baggage, so too are you and I oftentimes. Our prospects are stifled by stuff such as fear, doubt and anxiety. But even though Saul hid himself, the people "ran and fetched him thence. . . . And Samuel said to all the people, see ye him whom the LORD hath chosen . . . people shouted, and said, God save the king" (1 Samuel 10:23-24, *KJV*).

Just like Saul ran out of sight, I too hid myself among the baggage of fear when it came to taking a head coaching position, but ever since I fully believed who God told me that I am and stepped out in faith, I have come to realize the potential inside me. When you come out from the baggage and bondage of fear, doubt and anxiety, and humbly receive what God has for you, you will begin to see your hidden potential and realize that you are head and shoulders above the rest where you thought that you were less! God does not want for us to get off course amidst the baggage, or to carry around that heavy baggage. Instead He invites us to lay down all the heavy bags at the foot of the Cross and leave them there, even if we get tempted to pick them up again.

There is no one like you who can do what God called you to do. May you begin to see yourself the way God does. There is a king or queen inside of you waiting to reach his or her *full potential* if you will only believe in who God tells you that you are, and what God has placed inside of you! This is your time.

TIMEOUT
Read Psalm 50:5; Joshua 1:9;
Judges 20:18,23,28.

PRAYER TIME
Heavenly Father, help me to see myself the way You do. Remove the baggage from my life so that I can be released to reach my full potential. You have not given me a spirit of fear, but of power, love and a sound mind. So I am resolved to walk in my purpose, knowing that You have created me to be something special for Your glory! In Jesus' mighty name. Amen.

Clipboard Notes

_____

_____

_____

_____

Second Half
11:00

STRETCH, NOT STRESS

For the eyes of the LORD range throughout the earth to strengthen
those whose hearts are fully committed to him.

2 CHRONICLES 16:9 *(NIV)*

Warm-Up
We need to allow God to spiritually stretch us so that we are
prepared to handle the stresses of life.

Game Time

God wants to stretch you, not stress you! Before practice or a game, players stretch so that when the stress of the game comes, they are physically prepared to handle that stress. The same works with God. God desires to stretch us—to prepare our spiritual muscles for those times of stress that are a part of life.

Four months had passed of my first year as a head coach, and I found myself in a place of peace. It was a time when I could focus on what was really important. It was a time when I could allow God to spiritually stretch me so that I could sow into the lives of my players the things that would equip them for a lifetime of success in their everyday walk. And so I prayed that God would use the stress-free time to stretch me—to prepare my spiritual muscles so that when the stress of life came (and it always comes!), I would be prepared to live before my players in a way that honors God.

In coaching you will have stressful moments. In sports you will have stressful moments. The question is, how do you prepare for that stress? In your own strength, you can never adequately or fully handle the pressure. If you ever think that way, you are only fooling yourself. There will be times when the stress is like a tsunami, and your response will tell a lot about how well you've allowed the Lord to stretch you. Are your muscles ready, strengthened through Jesus Christ to respond to whatever stress you face? As coaches, we face the stress of competition, of players who don't always perform, of media who want answers, or the stress you put on yourself to succeed. By nature, we are competitive and that means stress, but muscles that have been lovingly stretched by nail-scarred hands are equipped and ready.

Consistency should be your nature just as it is the nature of who Christ is. You want to see consistency in your players. You want to know that they are stretched and ready for each game. That is Christ's desire for you as well. You will be consistent in your response to stress when you have been stretched ahead of time.

A great reminder: One of the greatest muscle-stretching truths that can prepare you for stress is to know that this is temporal. The day will come when your number of wins won't matter, your honors and achievements will fade, but your eternal investment in the lives of your players will remain. A. W. Tozer reminds us, "We must meet the uncertainties of this world with the certainty of the world to come." And the best way to do this is to be spiritually stretched by God so that you can play the game to His honor and glory.

TIMEOUT

Read Romans 8:17-18; Hebrews 13:20-21; 2 Corinthians 4:16-18.

PRAYER TIME

Lord, it isn't always comfortable to be stretched, but it's always worthwhile. Help me to remember that the hands that stretch me were stretched out for me on a cross. Thank You that those same hands are willing to prepare me for the stresses of life—to equip me to respond in a way that brings honor and glory to You. May I yield to Your times of stretching, so that I may honor You in the stress of the game. Amen.

 **Clipboard Notes**

_____

_____

Second Half

10:00

LOOK OUT BELOW

But he said to him, "Behold, there is a man of God in this city, and he is a man who is held in honor; all that he says comes true. So now let us go there. Perhaps he can tell us the way we should go."

1 SAMUEL 9:6 *(ESV)*

Warm-Up

God knows how to get to where you need to go—
and He will direct you as to how to get there.

Game Time

Saul was an impressive young man, and he grew up in an influential family that had a great amount of livestock and servants. One particular day, his family's donkeys wandered off, so Saul's father asked him and one of the attendants to go out to look for the donkeys. They went through several regions, but to no avail.

Saul finally decided that it was best to go back, otherwise his father would begin to worry about them rather than the donkeys. The attendant suggested that they go and speak with a man who might know where the donkeys were located. Just as the attendant had suspected, the man assured them that the donkeys had been found and were fine. The man invited Saul and his attendant to join him at a banquet, and they were given a place at the head of the table. At the banquet, Saul received valuable insight into his personal life, which was a tremendous blessing. Samuel had petitioned the Lord, and the Lord commanded Samuel to give the people a king. God led Saul to Samuel; Samuel anointed Saul king.

As the head coach, you are surrounded by people who are on different levels in the hierarchy of staffing—assistant coaches, secretaries, director of operations, managers—so you need to have a listening ear to hear what each one may have to say. It takes courage to always be the one on stage, but it takes humility to be still and listen. When you appreciate the unique talents and abilities of those you come in contact with—men and women who have a great reputation for their skills and faithfulness—the blessings dole out both ways. Those who are familiar with God and useful to the kingdom of God are truly honorable. Wherever you are in your journey, you can improve your opportunities of acquainting yourself with those who are wise and good in order to follow your purposeful course according to God's divine direction.

In the social structure, Saul's attendant would be considered the lower man on the totem pole because of his title, but "look out below"—because you never know who may have answers to questions, connections you may not have, invaluable insight, or solutions to a problem.

Good advice: As Jack Nichols said, "Every person I work with knows something better than me. My job is to listen long enough to find it and use it."

TIMEOUT
> Read Psalm 32:8; 1 Corinthians 1:25; John 10:4.

PRAYER TIME
Heavenly Father, You lead step by step and know the end from the beginning, because You alone are sovereign. I am Your instrument and I trust You as I take one step at a time, even though You do not reveal the destination right away. Mold me daily, almighty God, and order my steps so that I learn to follow only Your divine direction, whether through likely or unusual methods. Forgive me when I doubt or fear, and grow me in Your Spirit. In Jesus' mighty name. Amen.

 Clipboard Notes

_____

_____

Second Half
9:00

GOOD AND TEACH

"Neither do I condemn you," said Jesus.
"Go, and from now on do not sin anymore."
JOHN 8:11 *(CSB)*

Warm-Up
Through the lens of "Good and Teach," you
learn from your mistakes and grow.

Game Time

Every day has opportunities to improve, to build upon what you are already doing well. Growth often comes when you learn from your mistakes.

Everyone makes them; it is what you do after the fact that will determine whether the mistake will pull you deeper into a pit or push you closer to your created purpose.

This principle holds true for your team, you personally and your players—both as you prepare them for the next game and as you disciple them in life beyond your sport. At Elon, after each game our staff puts together selected video clips as part of what we call "Good and Teach." The "good" clips show solid performances, and the "teach" clips highlight what we need to improve upon. It makes sense that we would call our best moment "good," but then shouldn't we call our errors "bad"? To call something "bad" sounds condemning and judgmental, whereas "teach" sounds as if you have a vested interest in helping to correct what went wrong and to improve future performance. It is kinder, and you are more likely to get an enthusiastic response from your players. It is all about using the correct words.

Jesus used "good and teach." When He walked among us on Earth, His compassion for people allowed Him to identify errors in a way that provoked a desire for change rather than a desire to remain the same or to rebel. Receptive hearts in those He corrected also reduced the chances of the mistake being repeated.

Jesus went into "good and teach" mode when the Pharisees brought before Him a woman who had committed adultery. The crowd was ready to stone her to death because of her sin, but they wanted to see how the Messiah would react. He surprised them, and probably surprised the woman too.

Jesus invited anyone in the crowd who was without sin to throw the first stone at her. That brought on silence, and left the woman physically unscathed. The Pharisees began to disperse one after another, but Jesus remained with the woman.

Jesus did not throw a stone at the woman. I would call that a powerful teaching clip. He taught a lesson without scolding the Pharisees or declaring what they had done as being bad. Neither did He condemn the woman who had committed adultery. He simply said, "Go, and from now on do not sin anymore" (John 8:11). It was clear that she had made a mistake; but as far as Jesus was concerned, what she had done was in the past.

Likewise, your mistakes can be in the past. Jesus' "good and teach" message is for you too. Every day has opportunities. You can deepen your spiritual walk with Christ as you learn from your mistakes and correct them.

A good place to start: This book emphasizes prayer, yet you might struggle with finding time to talk with God. Rather than repeating the mistake again tomorrow and beating yourself up, take a look at how being without prayer hurts and how spending time with God helps. Through the lens of "good and teach," you might reprioritize prayer—and that perspective might help you find the time to talk with God each day.

TIMEOUT
Read John 8:2-11.

PRAYER TIME

Dear God, I acknowledge my mistakes, first, forgive me for my sins. Thank You for not condemning me but healing me instead. Please show me what I need to learn from my mistakes so that I will not repeat them but grow closer to You. Amen.

Clipboard Notes

_____

_____

_____

_____

_____

Second Half

08:00

MIGHTY IN BATTLE

*Who is this King of glory? The LORD, strong and mighty,
the LORD, mighty in battle.*

PSALM 24:8 *(NIV)*

Warm-Up

Just as the Lord is strong and mighty in battle, so you can be too.

Game Time

Every game, match or meet is a battle. In the arena or stadium, coaches live to face and triumph over an opponent. It is never enough to simply have athletes on your team who have the physical ability to throw a baseball, shoot a basketball or hit a tennis ball. Skill, strategy and preparedness get you into the game. But the strength to win with consistency comes from within. This is true in athletic competition and even more so in life beyond the game. B.A.T.T.L.E. is an acrostic I put together to help to illustrate the concept:

B=Believe that you are a winner. God's Word says that you are more than a conqueror through Christ Jesus (see Romans 8:37). This means that the real battles in your life have already been won because of the price that Jesus paid with His life.

A=Act like a winner. Goliath was a physically intimidating opponent, much stronger than David. During their epic confrontation, what did David do when Goliath and the Philistines moved forward to attack? David ran to the battle line! He was eager to face Goliath and acted like someone who could fell the big guy even before he slung the first stone (see 1 Samuel 17). When it comes to challenges, winners face them; they don't run away from them.

T=Talk like a winner. When David made up his mind to fight Goliath, he said, "Don't let anyone be discouraged by him; your servant will go and fight this Philistine!" (1 Samuel 17:32). David made it known that he feared no challenge! When you serve the true and living God, you can go into battle with great confidence.

T=Trust in your own abilities. When Saul found out that David was going to fight Goliath, he tried to help. Saul took off his own armor and offered it to David. Yet David could not use the armor because he could not walk while wearing it. David did have the ability to use a slingshot, and that was the perfect weapon to use to slay the giant.

L=Lean on people who will support you while you are in battle. When David's life was at stake, a man named Jonathan committed himself to David in order to support him. Jonathan told David, "Whatever you say, I will do for you." Their bond was so strong that they became best friends and confidants.

E=Enjoy the fruits of your labor. When you endure through and to the end of a battle, you will reap the benefits of God's promises to you. David pushed forward to victory and became king. He prospered and passed His blessings on to many generations.

It is worth repeating: For every promise there is a battle, but for every time that you endure and battle until the end, there is a blessing waiting for you. Be strong and mighty in battle!

TIMEOUT
Read 1 Samuel 17.

PRAYER TIME

Lord, you know the struggles and problems I face. Today I choose to
believe, act and talk like a winner because Your Son paid the price for
victory. Just like David declared, I also declare that all my battles belong to
You, Lord. Although I often feel as though I only have a slingshot,
I know that in You is the might to prevail. Amen.

Clipboard Notes

_____

_____

_____

_____

_____

Second Half
07:00

A HEART TRANSPLANT

I'll give you a new heart, put a new spirit in you. I'll remove the stone heart from your body and replace it with a heart that's God-willed, not self-willed.
EZEKIEL 36:26 *(THE MESSAGE)*

Warm-Up
You need to coach with heart, but the question is, with which heart?

Game Time
Some people say they wear their hearts on their sleeves. I guess I wear my heart on my sleeve and on my Facebook page. Knowing that players, opponents and everyone else can see what I post, I seek to be honest and to always point people toward God. Sometimes I am serious with my comments, at other times I have fun.

Our team at Elon was doing well as we entered the final weeks of the 2012-2013 season. We were positioned to be invited to a post-season tournament—and indeed we were invited to the Women's Basketball Invitational and won our first-round game.

Post-season basketball was not new for me. In 1993-1994, I played for the University of North Carolina. Our Tar Heel team was good. We went 33-2 and made it to finals. With the NCAA championship on the line, we battled a confident Louisiana Tech team. We trailed by one point as time was running out. The ball was in my hands.

An instant before the buzzer sounded, I shot the ball. I didn't look at it, and the mob of teammates celebrating our win got to me before I knew it had gone in. That was playing with heart as much as it was playing with physical skills. We needed both.

As our Elon team moved toward post-season, I knew the players had the heart and the physical skills to make a run. So it was a good time for me to check my own heart. Be careful when you ask

God to reveal your heart to you so that you can see it in the same way He sees it. Your heart may not be as pure as you thought it was.

You may give God thanks for giving you a team of unbelievably great players (I did), and you may ask Him for a humble heart during a time of success (I did). He will listen, but then He may have a concern about something altogether different—maybe even something much deeper. Get ready.

I had prayed such a prayer in the final weeks of the stellar season, and God revealed to me some things that I needed to change. I needed a heart transplant, and I asked everyone reading my Facebook posts to pray for me.

I had questions for myself. I posted these too, thinking that they might challenge others as well. If God asked you what is the desire of your heart, what would it be? Are your desires for earthly success greater than your desires for kingdom success? Would you want the wisdom of Solomon to lead God's people, or would you long for wealth and riches for your own earthly gain instead? Would you be honest with yourself?

Life is about learning. Every day God will teach you something if you have an open mind and a transplanted heart.

It all goes back to a truth you know: Seek first the kingdom of heaven and everything else shall be added unto you (see Matthew 6:33). What are you seeking? Is your heart truly in the right place? Or do you need a transplant too?

TIMEOUT
Read Psalm 51:10; Matthew 5:8.

PRAYER TIME
Dear Lord, examine my heart. Show it to me as You see it.
Reveal to me all that needs to be changed. Check my motives. Let me desire only what You desire, so that my desires will be pure. Let me desire only the things that will bring glory and honor to You, not myself. Let me become God-willed and not self-willed. Amen.

 Clipboard Notes

_____

_____

Second Half

06:00

THE COST OF LOYALTY

Do not persuade me to leave you or go back and not follow you.
For wherever you go, I will go, and wherever you live, I will live;
your people will be my people, and your God will be my God.

RUTH 1:16 *(CSB)*

Warm-Up

True loyalty is a two-way street.

Game Time

Naomi insisted that she was too old. Her husband had died. So had her two sons. Fearing that God was punishing her and concluding that no man would want to marry her, she gave up.

"Return home," Naomi told her two daughters-in-law. She kissed them and wept, but there was no longer a way to provide for their needs, which was the custom of that day.

Naomi believed she was acting in the best interests of the other women. One of her daughters-in-law thought otherwise. Ruth refused to leave. She clung to Naomi, and they traveled together to Bethlehem. Ruth was loyal.

Every professional development seminar I've ever attended has emphasized the importance of hiring a loyal staff. Recruits need to have the same character quality. When the going gets tough, the tough remain loyal.

Coaches know the importance of faithful, reliable, trustworthy, dedicated, steadfast and unwavering assistants and players. But how many see that for loyalty to work, it must be reciprocal? Commitment is a two-way street. You need to be just as loyal to the people around you as they are to you. What you value in others, you must first nurture in yourself. What you desire from others, you must first give to them.

What does loyalty look like to you?

The story of Naomi and Ruth took place at a time when famine had struck the land of Bethlehem, which forced Naomi and her family to leave for Moab. While in this strange land, both Naomi and Ruth lost their husbands.

When the famine was over, Naomi decided to return to Bethlehem. That's when she asked her daughters-in-law to go their separate ways. Was it a two-way street? Yes. Naomi had followed custom and provided, even through the famine. But when her possibilities diminished, she faithfully suggested that her daughters-in-law go to places where they could be helped. Ruth had adopted Naomi's people as her people and Naomi's God as her God, and she chose to stay. This is a story of loyalty at its best!

A deeper thought: Sometimes loyalty has a cost, but the result is worth the risk. Coach John Wooden once said, "No team or individual will become great without loyalty."

TIMEOUT
Read Deuteronomy 32:4; Psalm 89:8;
Psalm 177:1-2.

PRAYER TIME
Lord, help me to embody all that You are! A big part of who
You are is a God who is loyal, a God who is faithful. Equip me through
Your Holy Spirit to display this fruit of the Spirit: faithfulness—
also known as loyalty. Amen.

Clipboard Notes

_____

_____

_____

Second Half

05:00

MUSTARD SEED FAITH

And Saul said to David, Thou art not able to go against this Philistine to fight with him: for thou art but a youth, and he a man of war from his youth.
1 SAMUEL 17:33 *(KJV)*

Warm-Up

You can either accept a wrong opinion about you
or challenge it and prevail.

Game Time

David was told that he was too young to go to battle against Goliath. How many coaches have heard that said about them? How many players? I heard it said about me.

One thing I've learned is that lack of experience does not mean lack of ability. David had not enlisted in Saul's army as a soldier, but he had fought many battles while being a little shepherd boy that gave him more than enough confidence to go against Goliath.

I wasn't getting mailboxes full of invitations to coach. In fact, the door seemed to be shut. Three times in one year I was denied. What did I do? I just kept on knocking on doors. Finally, a door of opportunity opened at Elon University—and in the end I could see clearly that it was the right door, and worth the wait.

Finally somebody believed in me, just as I did—and just as God did. I can't say that it was big faith, but it was mustard seed faith that preceded my first head coaching job. The Bible says that if we have faith the size of a mustard seed then we can move mountains (see Matthew 17:20). I had just enough faith to do one more interview for a head coaching job.

I had a choice: I could accept the doubters' opinion of me or challenge it—just as in the game of football, when a coach feels that an official has made an incorrect ruling, he can accept it or challenge it. I decided that there was an incorrect ruling about my future. I knew that God was calling me to move forward in my career. When He calls, He also equips. I still had that little bit of faith inside pushing me to believe that I should challenge what others were saying.

A helpful hint: Don't allow people to dump their false projections on you. Don't allow anyone to marginalize you, write your story, or define you. Let God write your story—all it takes is faith the size of a mustard seed.

TIMEOUT

Read Psalm 31:15; Luke 17:6.

PRAYER TIME

Dear God, You know me better than anyone else, and You have established a purpose for my life. Rather than accept what people who don't know me say about me, I choose to let You define me. Rather than let others limit my future, I choose to let You write my story. Give me faith the size of a mustard seed so that the mountains separating me from Your purpose for my life will be removed. Amen.

Clipboard Notes

_____

_____

_____

_____

_____

Second Half

04:00

A REFLECTION OF YOU

He is the radiance of His glory and the exact representation of His nature.
HEBREWS 1:3 *(NASB)*

Warm-Up

When you look in the mirror, who do you see?

Game Time

"Come on, run the play!"

"We need better execution!"

"That is not how we taught it! I need you to run it exactly how I showed you!"

You are a coach. So you recognize these sentences. Perhaps you have used them—today!

In practice you teach and introduce players to the offensive plays you want to run. Then you repeatedly review the plays to make sure that everyone understands where, why and when they are supposed to be on the court. You know that as a coach, nothing is more frustrating than to have taught your players your philosophy, principles and concepts only to see most of it not being executed in the game. On some levels it's embarrassing because their lack of execution isn't so much their doing, but it is a reflection of you as a coach. You have to bear the responsibility.

On the flipside, a well-disciplined team that executes its plays with precision is also a reflection of the coach. Long-time Los Angeles Lakers Coach Phil Jackson's teams always believed in themselves—that mirrored Phil Jackson. Former St. Louis Cardinals manager Tony La Russa's teams were always prepared. That mirrored Tony La Russa.

The greatest playbook ever written is God's Word. It teaches us how to become a reflection of Him. You go to church on Sunday to hear the Word taught. The pastor gives you "plays" (Scripture verses) that are supposed to help you live more effectively for Christ each day.

Everything sounds nice at church (practice), yet when you step outside (the game of life), sometimes events don't transpire as you thought they would. When that happens, you should take a long look in the mirror to see whose reflection is there.

Are you a reflection of God's playbook in everyday living, or are you executing the plays in church only? God gives you plays to live by, plays to execute in order to create a better life, plays to bring glory to Him and to draw others unto Him.

A challenge worth pursuing: You are to be the exact representation of God—a reflection of Him in all that you do and say, so that your life is a testament about the God you serve. When you execute what God is calling you to do, and when you obey His Word, you become a reflection of the Father, the radiance of His glory, and the exact representation of His nature. There is no better way to live your life as a head coach.

TIMEOUT
Read 1 John 4:17.

PRAYER TIME

Lord, my heart's desire is to reflect You. When people see me, I want them to see You! Thank You for Your Word that guides me in all truth and shows me how to represent You in ways that will bring glory to Your name. Help me to execute Your plans and purpose for my life to perfection, so that I will be light that shines and displays Your nature before all my players. Amen.

Clipboard Notes

_____

_____

Second Half

03:00

A COVER-UP

Then David confessed to Nathan, "I have sinned against the LORD."

2 SAMUEL 12:13 *(NLT)*

Warm-Up

When you mess up, 'fess up.

Game Time

At Elon University, all of the head coaches and the athletic director gather once a month. We have a coach coaching the coaches session.

I remember the first meeting I attended as a head coach. Our athletic director, Dave Blank, talked about conducting ourselves in the right way, not only for the good of our individual reputations but also for the greater good. As coaches and employees, we are ambassadors for the university.

Dave noted several instances in which coaches at other schools had made mistakes—some had been handled well, others not so well. His conclusion: "When you mess up, 'fess up." That phrase has stuck with me.

It pays off in so many ways to follow Dave's advice, not only on the big blunders, but on the small gaffes too. Situations and relationships only get worse when you go into cover-up mode.

Too often when we make mistakes, our initial thought or response is to find a way to squirm our way out of it. How many times have you blamed someone else for something you did?

When you mess up, pause before you react. Remember that for every action there is a reaction. When you step outside the boundaries of what is right (whether it was your fault or not), there are always consequences.

You might be able to hide a mess-up from some people, even for a long period of time, but you can never hide it from God. Your mistake will eventually come to light.

Your actions not only affect you, but they also affect the people around you. When you fall short of God's glory, it's wise to follow the example of David. God called David a man after His own heart, not because he was perfect but because he was quick to recognize his mistakes, take responsibility for them, and ask for forgiveness.

A good way to avert a bigger mistake: Don't let the sun go down on your anger (see Ephesians 4:26). When you go to bed upset or cover up a mistake, it gives the devil a foothold. In other words, when angry, 'fess up and allow God to forgive you.

T I M E O U T

Read Psalm 32:5; Ephesians 4:26.

P R A Y E R   T I M E

Father, allow Your Holy Spirit to be the pricking conviction I need to avoid costly mistakes in my walk with You. I want to meditate on the things that are pure, true and holy so that my actions follow suit. Let not the sun go down on my anger. And help me to be like David, recognizing and confessing my sin—and quickly asking for Your forgiveness. Amen.

Clipboard Notes

_____

_____

_____

_____

_____

Second Half

02:00

NOT A SUBSTITUTE

Their idols are like scarecrows in a cucumber field, and they cannot speak;
they have to be carried, for they cannot walk. Do not be afraid of them, for
they cannot do evil, neither is it in them to do good.

JEREMIAH 10:5 *(ESV)*

Warm-Up

Are sports your idol? How about your job? Is it an idol?

Game Time

Dear America's Next Top Coach,

I would first of all like to congratulate you for allowing me to take the place of God. Now there is nothing standing in our way! We will watch game footage all day, fall asleep, and do it all over again! How exciting is that?

When you were devoting time to that other guy (I think His name is God, Jesus, Yahweh, Jehovah), you missed out on so much that I had to offer. Don't you know there are other coaches that have passed you by because they are more devoted; they give more of their time to becoming the next big thing in the basketball world?!

Man alive, you need to take a look at this new catalog that just came in the mail. Check out the hot website and order a few more of these instructional DVDs. Spend your entire weekend soaking it up—yes, including Sunday morning. Every second counts if you want to get ahead! We don't have time to waste, so those 41 devotional readings (more Jesus stuff) in Charlotte Smith's book that claim to draw you closer to God—forget about them! Add up all those minutes reading devotionals (and the time reading the Bible) over the year and you'll realize you could have gotten a few more phone calls in, written a few more letters to recruits, or sent a few more text messages to those underclassmen. Oops, did I say text messages? Well you know a few here and there haven't ever hurt anybody, have they? Anyway, I'm just glad you have finally come to your senses. Now we can eat, sleep and breathe this job. Work is our priority and we don't have time to waste. Worship me and I'll take you places, kiddo!

Sincerely,

Your Idol, Sports

Doesn't it all sound so tempting? You start with right motives, even knowing that God has placed you in a strategic place in the world and that is the world of sports. Then the pressure mounts.

You see the workaholic at that other school or coaching that other team who bends some rules and commits every second to the passion of succeeding. Soon enough, you are consumed and your sport has become an idol. This is not to be confused with dedication, hard work and success—those all can and should be pursued.

But nothing—no sport, job, hobby or person—can ever take the place of God as Lord. Once you have discovered that God has a plan and purpose for you through your role as coach, you will experience a joy that will endure. Your love for coaching will be maximized when you discover that coaching is a call from God to invest in the lives of people. The joy of serving God as a coach has great rewards. It is the conviction of God's call and the opportunity to invest in lives for eternal purposes that carries you through the ups and downs, wins and losses.

It is too easy to get consumed with the need to win—to the point where you lose your perspective and come to a place of over-indulgence of self. You worry that if you don't win, you won't have a job, you won't land the top recruit, or the fans will not like you. These worries drive you to a place of fear, even terror.

When you start to operate out of fear, you find yourself operating out of desperation—that's when you know that your sport has become an idol. Desperation causes you to convince yourself that wrong is right. Don't reach that point. Trust that just as God gave you your job, He also will sustain you.

A helpful hint: God has to be the star, the key player on your team in the game of your life. He cannot be a substitute coming off the bench. He is the go-to player. And He gets all the glory.

God has given you an assignment; and it's not just a job to make money to pay your bills.

TIMEOUT

Read Hosea 14:8; 1 Corinthians 12:2;
1 John 5:21.

PRAYER TIME

Dear Lord, thank You for giving me my position as a coach. Let me remember that, because it is an assignment from You, I can trust You to lead me and guide me. Don't let me ever make sports an idol, but give me the dedication and drive to excel for You. In Jesus' name. Amen.

Clipboard Notes

_____
_____
_____
_____
_____

Second Half

01:00

BECOMING A REAL CHAMPION

The thief comes only to steal and kill and destroy.
I came that they may have life and have it abundantly.

JOHN 10:10 *(ESV)*

Warm-Up

You are forever a champion in Christ.

Game Time

In this life, you will always have an opponent. His name is Satan and his mission is to steal, kill and destroy you. But do not worry, because you have a teammate who wants you to live out an abundant life.

When you accept Jesus Christ as your personal Savior, you become part of a winning team. You join a dynasty that will never lose, because God's kingdom has no end. This means that your winning streak will never be broken. You are forever a champion in Christ.

Players on a winning team exhibit a certain mentality. They simply don't accept defeat. They never say die. Because they believe they are the best team, they deem winning as rightfully theirs.

Abundant life is rightfully yours because that is what Christ desires for you to have. You have to want to have it just as much as He wants to give it to you. You have to be willing to go one on one with Satan's schemes and let the devil know that no matter what his tactics are, you will not give up—you will not be destroyed.

Second Corinthians 4:8-9 says, "We are hard pressed on every side, but not crushed; perplexed, but not in despair; persecuted, but not abandoned; struck down, but not destroyed" (*NIV*).

Yes, the enemy will put a full-court press on you at times and try to wear you down in your thought life, in unforeseen circumstances, in worry, doubt and fear. But you must stand firm in your faith and use God's Word as your press breaker.

When you are trapped by one of the devil's schemes, make the outlet pass to 2 Timothy 1:7, which says, "For God has not given us a spirit of fearfulness, but one of power, love, and sound judgment." Have your game plan ready to defeat your opponent by equipping yourself with the Word of God so that you can have life and have it more abundantly. When you do this, you are a real champion.

TIMEOUT
Read Proverbs 21:31; Ephesians 6:12.

PRAYER TIME
Lord, thank You that I will forever be a champion in You.
Help me to realize and to remember who I am in You when the battle
gets tough. Thank You that the battle has already been won for me. and
that all I have to do is stand firm on Your Word. I will not give up.
I will not cave in. I am victorious and I will fight until the end, because
with You, I am on the winning side all the time! Amen.

Clipboard Notes

_____

_____

_____

_____

_____

End of Regulation Time
At the Buzzer

00:00

HOW WILL YOU BE REMEMBERED?

At that time those who feared the LORD spoke to one another. The LORD took notice and listened. So a book of remembrance was written before Him for those who feared Yahweh and had high regard for His name.

MALACHI 3:16 *(CSB)*

Warm-Up
Your legacy is about more than what happens in the game.
It is also about what happens beyond the game.

Game Time

Malachi 3:14-15 contrasts the righteous and the wicked. There were some believers who were discouraged because it seemed as though the wicked were prospering, unlike the righteous. They felt it was useless to serve God, because it seemed as though they were not gaining anything from Him. These believers began to speak harshly about God.

A few of the righteous believers feared the Lord and had high regard for His name despite their circumstances. Their words of support caught the Lord's attention and their faithfulness pleased Him, so a book of remembrance was written—a record of the remnant's steady commitment to God.

In sports, it is tempting to try to keep up with Coach Jones. But you are not called to follow after every trend; rather, you are called to walk in integrity. Be assured, the Lord takes notice of those who fear Him. It is a reverential fear in which you operate in a spirit of excellence just as Christ walked in honesty. When you act in this manner, you will be written in a book of remembrance for standing your ground.

As a coach, how will you be remembered? Will you transform the world by walking in integrity, or will you conform to the ways of the wicked? How will you be remembered?

One day when I was a little girl, my brothers were in the other room watching TV. At one point, I heard a big commotion from my brothers, so I decided to run into the living room to see what had caught their attention. As I scampered through the house, unfortunately I ran into an iron that was sitting on a table. To this day you can still see an iron impression on my thigh from where I was severely burned. It left a mark.

Think about this: Every time you compete, coach or lead, you leave an imprint. Whether it is a positive or a negative impression is up to you. When you are committed to excellence, you naturally desire to leave the kind of mark on others that will have an eternal impact for their good. So you have to make sure that you are a good coach.

A closing thought and challenge: I once heard a quote that went something like this: "Sports is about changing lives and creating better human beings through competition and training. Winning games is easy; changing lives is legendary."

What do you want your legacy to be?

TIMEOUT

Read Ecclesiastes 2:21; Matthew 25:21-23.

PRAYER TIME

Father, help me to focus on that which is eternal so that I will always keep the right perspective in life. I will keep my eyes on You so that I will follow Your will and not the world. What I gain by following You wholeheartedly and completely is all that matters. Amen.

 **Clipboard Notes**

_____

_____

Acknowledgments

ANGELS ALONG THE WAY

*Having mentors that surround you with godly advice
is like having angels along this journey of life.
They instruct you as to what is best by saying, "Take this road."
They point you to the way in which you need to go,
Sometimes they give a forceful push, sometimes a gentle nudge;
They always do what's best for you because of their undying love.
So I would be completely remiss if I did not take the time to say,
"Lord, I thank You for all my angels along the way."*

CHARLOTTE D. SMITH

I dedicate this book to my loving Father above, from whom all my help comes. God, I thank You for choosing me to be a vessel for Your glory. Thank You for my loving father and mother, Ulysses Smith Jr. and Etta Smith, who trained me up in the way that I should go so that I would not depart from Your loving arms. I pray that both of them are smiling down from heaven and celebrating this amazing milestone with me. Thank you, Mom and Dad, for giving me unconditional love and for showing me what family means.

I am grateful for my brothers Chad, Brian and Bernard, who all played a major role in helping me become the person I am and the player I was. I love you with all my heart. You all mean the world to me. You guys are my heartbeat. You made me strong! I can still beat you all 1 on 1 . . . smile!

To my stepmom, Falonda—I thank you for who you are! You have been an inspiration to me. Seeing you write your own book was a great motivation to me. Thank you for stepping in and filling the void in my father's life after the passing of my mom. You stood by my father and loved him against great opposition. I thank you for standing, because it was you he needed through the struggles he endured before he went on to be with the Lord. Out of your wonderful marriage, I was blessed with two beautiful sisters and a brother: Kendra Sullivan, Patricia Sullivan and Ulysses Smith III. I love you guys!

Perry Maison, when God sent you to be my godfather, He sent an angel to stand in the gap for me. I needed an earthly father, and God sent me the best. Thank you for loving me as your own. Thank you for encouraging me and equipping me through the Word of God! I will never forget the day before my press conference, after I had accepted the job at Elon University, when I was praying that I would have someone there to support me. When I got to the press conference, you were there like a proud father on the front row, along with my sister, Tonya Jackson. Thank you both for that!

A very special thank-you to my uncle and 1996 Basketball Hall of Famer, David "Skywalker" Thompson—you are my hero! I love you. I love your heart. You are an amazing man. A lot of people love you because of what you've accomplished; I love you simply for who you are! I look forward to the day when I can be a blessing to you as you have been a blessing to so many in our family.

And to Alvin Gentry, my cousin, because of your experience as a head coach in the NBA, your mentorship of me during my first year as a head coach was invaluable. Your wisdom and knowledge were a great blessing to me. Thank you.

To my junior-high track and field and high-school basketball coach, Howard McCleod: I can't thank you enough for what you poured into me. I remember our warm-ups before practices ever started—running over a mile to and through the graveyard, then back, and topping it off with those "6 inches" (leg raises). You made me so mentally tough. I thank you that you did not let superstars write their own rules. You taught me respect for authority, and you were no pushover—that kind of training is missing today, and I thank you for giving it, because I am better for it.

A special thank-you to my alma mater, the University of North Carolina! Thanks to all the scholarship donors who have made it possible for student athletes to excel both on and off the court. Thank you to my adopted mom and dad, Coach Sylvia Hatchell and Coach Andrew Calder. Thank you for believing in me! And I would be remiss if I didn't say thanks, Coach Fred Applin, for recruiting me. All of you are so much more than coaches to me. You have been there for me through the loss of both my parents, you were there on the day I got married, and you were there for me through the tough times in the loss of my marriage. I will forever be grateful to God that our paths crossed. And to all my Hoop-Phi sisters—I love you guys for life!

To all my people in Shelby, North Carolina. This is where it all started! A big shout-out to Robertsdale and the playground where it all went down. This is where my skills were developed, playing with the boys and my Phillips sisters!

Sometimes it's hard for me to express in words how grateful I am to God for sending me to Elon University. I can't say enough good things about the university and the people there. It's those people who won my heart. I once said that if I were ever to leave UNC, it would have to be for a special place—I found that in Elon. Thank you to President Leo Lambert, Gerry Francis, Dave Blank, Faith Shearer, Kyle Wills and Dr. Earl Danieley for believing in me! Thank you to all the fans of Elon Women's Basketball as well! I love Elon! The future is so bright there that people will need sunglasses to see it all unfold!

A very special thank-you to Robert Walker for the push I needed to pursue this dream and make it become a reality! Thank you for believing in me!

Thank you to Rob Williams. Your cover design is strong. It captures the message of the book. And your patience working with this first-time author is appreciated. Glad you are part of the team.

To my beloved editor, Steve Lawson—where, oh, where would I be without you? I thank God for you and for your commitment to *When Coaches Pray*. I thank God for your wisdom and insight to help make this book come to fruition. I hope this is just the beginning for us!

I know there are some forgotten ones whom I may have left out—charge it to my head, not my heart! Love ya!

ABOUT THE AUTHOR

Charlotte D. Smith is the head women's basketball coach at Elon University in Elon, North Carolina. She led the Phoenix to a 16-14 mark in her first season, the most victories by a first-year head coach in program history. In her second season, the Phoenix improved their record to 19-14 and went to the second round of post-season play.

As an assistant coach at the University of North Carolina for 9 seasons before arriving at Elon, Charlotte helped lead the Tar Heels to a 257-54 record, including a 100-30 mark in the Atlantic Coast Conference. UNC won 4 ACC titles during Charlotte's tenure, making 7 appearances in the top-25 national rankings. The Tar Heels made the NCAA Tournament all 9 seasons during Charlotte's tenure, making 2 trips to the Final Four as well as 6 Sweet 16 and 4 Elite Eight appearances.

The most decorated player in North Carolina history, Charlotte played for the Tar Heels from 1992 to 1995 and is one of only two UNC women's basketball players to have had her jersey retired. The 6-foot forward who wore No. 23 was named National Player of the Year by ESPN in 1995 following a career in which she scored 2,094 points (fifth all-time at UNC) and grabbed 1,200 rebounds (second all-time at UNC).

Charlotte is perhaps best known for her performance in the 1994 NCAA Championship game, when her buzzer-beating 3-pointer gave UNC the national crown with a 60-59 win over Louisiana Tech. She also had a championship-record 23 rebounds in the game and was named the Final Four's Most Outstanding Player. The ACC Rookie of the Year in 1992, Charlotte earned All-ACC and ACC Tournament MVP honors in her junior and senior seasons as the Tar Heels claimed back-to-back conference crowns.

As a senior, Charlotte was named All-America by Kodak, the Associated Press and the U.S. Basketball Writers Association. In 2002, she was named to the ACC's fiftieth anniversary team as one of the top players in conference history. She also was honored as the tenth-best female athlete in the history of the league. Early in her senior season, she became just the second collegiate women's player to dunk in a game when she did so against North Carolina A&T on December 4, 1994.

Following her collegiate career, Charlotte played professional basketball in Italy, where she was MVP of the Italian All-Star Game for the 1995-1996 season. She also spent the 1999-2000 season there. The Colorado Xplosion picked Charlotte in the third round (seventeenth overall) of the initial American Basketball League draft in 1996. She spent two-and-a-half seasons in the league, playing for Colorado and the San Jose Lasers and earning All-Star honors.

Charlotte was the thirty-third pick in the 1999 WNBA draft and played 6 seasons for the Charlotte Sting before moving to Washington in 2005 and then to Indiana in 2006. She has made numerous international appearances for US teams and was MVP of the 1996 USA Basketball Jones Cup squad, which won a gold medal. She also played for the 1997 USA Basketball Women's International Invitational team, the 1995 World University Games team, the 1994 US Select Team, the 1993 US Olympic Festival South team, and the 1992 Junior World Championship Qualifying team.

A native of Shelby, North Carolina, Charlotte graduated from Shelby High School, where she earned all-state honors and was her team's MVP all 4 years. Charlotte completed her UNC bachelor's degree in sociology in 1999. In addition to playing professional basketball, she interned in the Sting offices and worked for US Sports Management, Inc.

For more information about *Coaches Who Pray* contact coacheswhopray@gmail.com.

If you are interested in having Charlotte D. Smith speak at your event, meeting, school or church, contact US Sports at 704-821-2940.

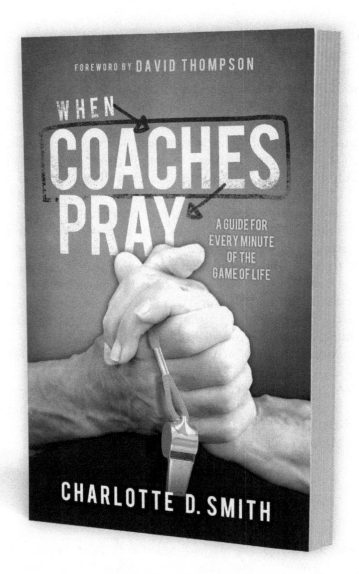

To order more copies of *When Coaches Pray* visit
www.thecoremediagroup.com

CPSIA information can be obtained
at www.ICGtesting.com
Printed in the USA
FSHW021657220520
70391FS